Fighting the Noonday Devil

Fighting the Noonday Devil

— AND OTHER ESSAYS PERSONAL AND THEOLOGICAL

R. R. Reno

WILLIAM B. EERDMANS PUBLISHING COMPANY
GRAND RAPIDS, MICHIGAN / CAMBRIDGE, U.K.

Published 2011 by
Wm. B. Eerdmans Publishing Co.
2140 Oak Industrial Drive N.E., Grand Rapids, Michigan 49505 /
P.O. Box 163, Cambridge CB3 9PU U.K.

Printed in the United States of America

16 15 14 13 12 11 7 6 5 4 3 2 1

ISBN 978-0-8028-6547-2

www.eerdmans.com

To Neal Kozodoy

and in memory of

Richard John Neuhaus

Contents

Introduction

Sitting in an apartment off Thirty-third Street a few blocks east of Johns Hopkins University in the summer of 1980, listening to a rambling political discussion, I could hear a police siren wailing gently in the distance. The summer heat and humidity were their usual stifling worst. With windows thrown open in the futile hope of capturing nonexistent cooling breezes, I could vaguely pick up the sound of Chuck Thompson, "the voice of the Baltimore Orioles," from a radio in a nearby apartment.

The Soviet Union had invaded Afghanistan the year before. Among other attempts at forceful reaction the ill-fated Jimmy Carter decided to require young men to register for the draft. For a person of my generation, the very word "draft" conjured up romantic, Vietnam-era images, and I committed myself to the great cause (at least in my late adolescent mind) of Resistance. So, in the early weeks of that summer, I spent a number of evenings with this haphazard crew of activists, producing leaflets and posters and sitting through long, futile meetings to discuss strategies for convincing eighteen-year-olds to refuse to register.

I no longer remember exactly how I came to be a part of that oddball group. No doubt somebody at Haverford College, where I had just completed my freshman year, knew about the antiwar crowd in Baltimore, and I was pointed in their direction. I had no real political views, and certainly no clear ideas about the Soviet Union or Afghanistan, or even war for that matter. So vague was my mind about such things that while a high school student I had met with coaches to talk about the possibility of playing lacrosse at West Point or Annapolis. I did, however, have an intense desire to be committed to a heroic cause, and for a young college student who came of age in the 1970s, being antidraft, antiwar, *antisystem* had become the standard and conventional gesture of moral earnestness.

In the hot apartment off Thirty-third Street, I was only half attentive as the discussion drifted toward speculation about the great and much hoped for revolution. I was sinking into a stuffed chair, the seat springs of which had long ago collapsed, relaxing myself into one of those horribly bent positions that are only comfortable for plastic, youthful spines. Phrases of the conversation, urgently enunciated in what seemed a well-practiced choreography of themes and ideas, drifted languidly through my daydreaming head. "Urban uprising" — "Police overreaction" — "Politicize the working class" — "Control of the urban core" — "Collapse of the capitalist system" — "An opening for revolutionary leadership."

My unfocused mind, so eager to take a stand, so romanced by causes, so enflamed by ideals, so committed to *doing* something, began to fix itself on a concrete thought. I made one of my rare interventions. From deep down in the old chair, I asked, "Shouldn't we be encouraging people in the city to plant gardens?" The four or five others turned and looked at me with surprise. I added, with hesitation, "I mean, if we really do spark an urban revolution and the capitalist economy collapses, then the whole system for food delivery and distribution in the city will collapse with it. Won't people need food?"

Nobody said anything. They looked at me with expressions of disbelief that I would interject practical irrelevancies into a discussion of revolutionary politics. After a second or two of silence they turned away and resumed their animated discussion. I heard the distant roar of the crowd at Memorial Stadium toward the east on Thirty-third Street. The faint voice of Chuck Thompson on the radio was joyfully announcing in a spirited tone of partisan enthusiasm that Eddie Murray had just hit a three-run homer. I shuddered inwardly as I vaguely sensed a distasteful moral truth that would take me years to discern and articulate to myself — the callous, theory-infected, inhumane abstractions of my fellow activists.

I soon dropped out of the feeble resistance movement, more because of a generally demoralized attitude brought on by the increasingly painful difference between the earnest rhetoric of the leaders and their limited competence as organizers than by any deep insights into the nature of politics, war, or resistance. Without thought or purpose or any particular intention, I blended back into the usual college student summer routines of indifferent jobs and pitchers of cheap National Bohemian Beer with buddies in the evenings at Jerry's Bar on Belvedere Avenue.

THE ODD COMBINATIONS of that long-ago summer haven't gone away. Endless books, all sorts of ideas, concepts, and theories, long academic lectures and freewheeling, late-night debates — the moral, spiritual, and intellectual ferment that led me to that ineffectual group of antiwar activists remains a central part of my life. In fact, by virtue of my vocation as a college professor I've quite naturally (and happily) become an evangelist of sorts for the sharp spurs and goads that help move us toward the examined life. We are not meant to leave things as they are; God commanded Adam and Eve to till and keep the garden, to exercise dominion. Society and the soul need to be subjected to a constant, cultivating scrutiny: Are we living as we should? It's not a question that can be easily answered, and therefore we're duty-bound to draw on all the intellectual resources at our disposal to try to formulate a humane answer, a true answer.

One crucial resource is the remarkable human capacity for abstraction and formal analysis. We can notice the local customs of other societies, and even make a catalogue of different forms: tea ceremonies in Japan, Samoan rituals of initiation, Swedish methods for mediating conflict, and so forth. In order to think accurately about how to live, we need detailed information about the world, fact-fortified with nuanced observation. Yet more powerful still is the capacity to theorize. When we formulate a concept of ceremony and ritual, or a cross-cultural model for analyzing conflict, then we furnish ourselves with extraordinarily powerful tools for thinking about what it means to be human. When we see the anatomy of reality — the muscles and bones and metabolic systems of culture — then we can more effectively diagnose our existential sicknesses.

There is nothing uniquely modern about the move toward theory and abstraction. Thucydides did not simply report on the Peloponnesian War; he analyzed motives and dissected tactics, all against the background of an implicit theory of social behavior. The book of Proverbs features the allegory of Lady Wisdom and Dame Folly, an imaginative and poetic expression of what amounts to a theory of the moral life. Our love is our weight, as Saint Augustine would say centuries later.

Ortega y Gasset once wrote against the theoretical impulse: "To create a concept is to leave the world behind." I began in college as a physics major, and although I've changed direction, I've never adopted a reactionary stance that rejects the indispensable power of theory. Our ability to enter into abstractions and use concepts allows us to see life not just as a series of instances, but also as a web of relations. Reality has an architecture, and we benefit from discerning its structural principles.

Some of the essays in this volume are exercises in theory. As I try to show in "Fighting the Noonday Devil," we need to see our postmodern era as animated by a spirit of self-protection, a desire to achieve a modicum of invulnerability to the existential pressures that threaten to take over our lives. As a result, the basic function of culture — to intrude upon the inner sanctum of soul and shape our desires, our hopes, our aspirations — becomes a threat that we fend off with intellectual techniques of critique and a general disposition of ironic detachment. It's an analysis I've undertaken on many occasions: my sociology of our sociological age. Indeed, so indebted am I to this theoretical diagnosis of our theoretical impulse that in the final essay, "The Intellectual Vocation," I provide a critical discussion of the limits of critical analysis. The upshot is a conceptually driven argument for the priority of love and loyalty over concept and critique.

There is no contradiction in criticizing the critics, any more than the effort to use close reasoning to show the limits of reason somehow controverts or undermines itself. But there is a temptation, which is why this volume of essays tilts heavily in the direction of memory, narrative, and episode rather than argument and analysis. The sheer power of concepts, their ability to illuminate the structures of reality, can bewitch. We search for a magical key, a general theory, a philosopher's stone of the intellect that will turn the vast heterogeneity of life into the filigreed gold of a comprehended coherence. We hope for vision that will give us mastery, and through mastery release, release from the need to return again and again and again to the question of how to live. Intoxicated with the promise of theory, addicted to vain images of its intellectual triumph, thirsting for the answer that will put an end to the agonies of our always unfolding responsibilities, we can forget that the web of life is constituted by relations between real people and real events.

So, yes, of course race, class, gender, and any number of other conceptually elaborated structures of culture and reality shape people's lives, but these and other aspects of the architecture of our humanity do not absorb or exhaust. On the contrary, the concrete particularity of life shimmers with the power of reality, a power that always overflows and floods our concepts with more than we can theorize. This is especially true of the recalcitrant and irritating, seductive and captivating uniqueness of human personality. "Persons influence us," John Henry Newman observed, "voices melt us, looks subdue us, deeds inflame us." When it comes to life, the longing, aching, searching poetry of the Song of Songs expresses the deepest architecture, the most fundamental logic. We are made for love. Any serious attempt to answer the question of how to live that ignores this primitive fact makes a mockery of reason and threatens to pervert and destroy our humanity.

A. G. Sertillanges, a Dominican and Thomist who lived in the early twentieth century, once wrote: "Truth serves only her slaves." The critical intellect dissects the world, in itself a worthy undertaking. But the pious intellect is greater. It allows the object of devotion to dissect the soul. Love renders us, and thus does the truth of things enter the fortified walls of our hearts as the power of renovation. It is in this spirit that I offer these essays. They are fragments of life, translucent at best, and often opaque. Ideas, concepts, theories, and all the other intellectual artifacts of our critical age and its drive toward understanding play roles. I am, after all, a professor. Yet in the main I have tried to serve what is real with words rather than dissect it with ideas, seeking to write with the disposition of love and loyalty, allowing what happens, what people say and do, what I have thought and others have written to work their ways into my mind.

I don't doubt that my efforts sometimes fail. The essays about youthful adventures may reflect the deceptive, distorting, false, and self-complimenting light that our mind projects onto reality and then relishes as discovery. The accounts of my spiritual trials undoubtedly end up serving my preconceived theological notions. Nonetheless, I hope readers will indulge these inevitable failures and take from them their proper lesson. We should beware living our ideas (even and perhaps especially our theological ideas) rather than our lives. And in living our lives we should recognize that the most fundamental task — and the most difficult task, especially for the modern, theoretically sophisticated intellectual — is the preparation of our hearts. The truth shines from the outside. The first step toward understanding requires removing the obstacles within; the final step involves the giving of oneself in the matrimony of assent. Everything else — the machinery of investigation, experiment, argument, and analysis — is commentary.

EARLIER VERSIONS of these essays appeared in the following journals and books: "Fighting the Noonday Devil," "Out of the Ruins," and "The End of the Road" in *First Things* (2003, 2005, 2008); "Faith in the Flesh," "Roughnecking It," and "Descent in the Dark" in *Commentary* (2007 and 2008); "The Intellectual Vocation" under a different title in *Gained Horizons: Regensburg and the Enlightenment of Reason,* ed. Bainard Cowan (2010).

Fighting the Noonday Devil

For most of the modern era, Christian apologists have emphasized the role of pride as the cardinal sin and primary barrier to faith. Milton's poetic vision is exemplary. At the outset of *Paradise Lost,* Milton describes the scene of fallen angels. Satan, their leader, rallies his troops with a speech justifying their rebellion. Bidding farewell to the "happy Fields" now lost, Satan hails the "infernal world," promising his followers that they, with him, might make "Heav'n of Hell." What seems a disaster can be made a victory. Satan's reasoning is simple. "Here at least," he says, "we shall be free." "Here," he continues, "we may reign secure." The gain, then, is autonomy and self-possession. Thus, in famous words, Milton has Satan pronounce the purest formula of pride: "Better to reign in Hell, than to serve in Heav'n."

To a great extent, the standard story of modernity emphasizes exactly the self-confidence and self-assertion that Milton describes in *Paradise Lost.* We all know the way the story is told. The emerging powers of modern science gave the seventeenth and eighteenth century a keen sense of the real powers of the human intellect. Rebelling against servile obedience to dogmatic and clerical authority, progressive forces in Enlightenment culture championed free and open inquiry. The same sentiment, this standard story continues, characterizes modern moral and political thought. Against traditional moral ideals and social forms, modern thinkers have sought, and continue to seek, a pattern of life derived from and properly expressive of our humanity. Thus, Ralph Waldo Emerson shouts the battle cry of modernity: "Trust thyself." Against subservience to standards imposed by society, Emerson writes, "Nothing is at last sacred but the integrity of your own mind." So central and important is this self-affirmation that Emerson famously reports, "If I am the Devil's child, I will then live from the Devil." Better to reign in the hell of self-affirmation than to subordinate the self to alien ideals and remote principles, no matter how heavenly.

This voice of rebellion against God's sovereignty endures. Yet, in the twilight of modernity, do most of the people who buy books that trash the Christian tradition do so because they have vibrant Emersonian souls? Do the naysayers and critics of Christianity today attract audiences of willful and self-assertive individualists who are eager to find leverage to free themselves from the constraining powers of dogma and priestcraft? Does secularism today stem from a deep self-trust and demonic pride?

I am increasingly convinced that the answer to these questions is no. Pride may go before the fall. However, after the fall, other spiritual temptations and difficulties predominate. In our times, whether we call the prevailing outlook late modern or postmodern, the vigor and ambition of the ideal of self-reliance have lost their luster. When the United States Army can adopt a fine Emersonian sentiment — "Be all you can be" — as a recruiting slogan, then surely what was once a fresh challenge has become a familiar, worn-out cliché. For this and other reasons we need to turn our attention away from pride and look elsewhere for the deeper sources of contemporary resistance to the Christian message.

LOOKING ELSEWHERE does not mean looking away from the Christian tradition. Christians have not always thought pride the deepest threat to faith. For the ancient spiritual writers of the monastic movement, spiritual apathy was far more dangerous. Recalling the sixth verse of Psalm 91, the desert fathers wished to guard against "the sickness that lays waste at mid-day." Evagrius of Pontus, a fourth-century monk, is one of the earliest sources of information about the desert monastic movement, and he reports that gluttony, avarice, anger, and other vices threaten monastic life. Yet, of all these afflictions, he reports, "the demon of *acedia* — also called the noonday demon — is the one that causes the most serious trouble of all."

"Acedia" is a word of Greek origin that means, literally, "without care." In the Latin it is often translated as *tristitia* or *otiositas,* sadness or idleness. In English, this vice shows up in the standard lists of the seven deadly sins under the heading of sloth. But citing synonyms and translations only signals the crudest definitions. For the monastic tradition, acedia or sloth is a complex spiritual state that defies simple definition. It describes a lassitude and despair that overwhelm spiritual striving. Sloth is not mere idleness or laziness; it involves a *torpor animi,* a dullness of the soul that can stem from restless, distracted activity just as easily as from indolence and apathy. Bernard of Clairvaux speaks of a *sterilitas animae,* a sterility, dryness, and barrenness of his soul that makes the sweet honey of psalm singing seem tasteless and turns late-night vigils into empty trials. Medieval English writers often speak of acedia as wanhope, a waning of confidence in the efficacy and importance of prayer. In his depiction of the fourth ledge on the Mountain of Purgatory in the *Divine Comedy,* Dante describes those afflicted by acedia as suffering from *lento amore,* a slow love that cannot motivate and uplift, leaving the soul stagnant, unable to move under the heavy burden of sin.

Across these different accounts, a common picture emerges. The noonday devil tempts us into a state of spiritual despair and sadness that drains us of our Christian hope. It makes the life of prayer and charity seem pointless and futile. In the heat of mid-day, as the monk tires and begins to feel that the commitment to desert solitude was a terrible miscalculation, the demon of acedia whispers despairing and debilitating thoughts. "Did God intend for human beings to reach for the heavens?" "Does God really need our prayers?" "Aren't solitude and chastity unnatural and life denying?" According to another ancient writer in the Evagrian tradition, the noonday demon "stirs the monk also to long for different places in which he can find easily what is necessary for his life and can carry on a much less toilsome and more expedient profession. It is not on account of locality, the demon suggests, that one pleases God. He can be worshipped anywhere. . . . Thus the demon employs all his wiles so that the monk may leave his cell and flee from the race-course."

Are these temptations that afflict the monk as strange or alien as the unfamiliar Greek word *acedia?* I think not. Let me update the whispering voice of sloth: "All things are sanctified by the Lord, and one could just as well worship on the golf course as in a sanctuary made by human hands." Or: "God is love, and love affirms; therefore, God accepts me just as I am. I need not exercise myself to change." Or: "We should not want to put God in a box, so the Christian tradition must be seen as a resource for our spiritual journeys, not as a mandatory itinerary. I can pick and choose according to my own spiritual needs." Or: "Ardent conviction and intensely held beliefs are the source of violence. I'll be a better, more tolerant person if I relax a bit and take an approach to faith that is a bit more critical, a bit more lighthearted."

In our day, these temptations seem far more common and dangerous than Emerson's now conventional "trust thyself." After all, how many people, believers or unbelievers, wish to reign anywhere, either in heaven, or in hell, or even in their own souls? Few, I imagine. Most of us just want to be left alone so that we can get on with our lives. Most of us want to be safe. We want to find a cocoon, a spiritually, psychologically, economically, and physically gated community in which to live without danger and disturbance. The carefree life, a life *a-cedia,* is our cultural ideal. Pride may be the root of all evil, but in our day, the trunk, branches, and leaves of evil are characterized by a belief that moral responsibility, spiritual effort, and religious discipline are empty burdens, ineffective and archaic demands that cannot lead us forward. In our hearts we fear that faith commits us to inaccessible ideals that, even if we believe in them, reach beyond our capacity. We often want to believe, but just as often we shrink from sharp-edged dogmatic convictions that we all too easily imagine cutting and slashing and damaging our fragile egos.

ACEDIA, THEN, is a real threat, a deadly sin doing its deadly work in the present age. Its presence can be seen rather clearly in two important features of contemporary intellectual and moral culture. Consider, first, the intellectual spirit of dispassion and coolness that grows out of the ideal of "critical distance." This ideal often contributes to the *torpor animi* that afflicts any who have entered into the habituating practices of our universities. For many of our professors, the drama of education should break the magic spell of immediacy. Just as the commonsense observation that the sun revolves around the earth is quite false and needs to be corrected, so, we are told, we should step back from the moral and social opinions we were taught as children. Nothing given should be simply accepted. We must question our inherited assumptions and see them as being, at best, merely true-for-us rather than being simply true.

To spur us toward a self-doubting stance, contemporary education often turns into a form of cultural shock therapy. Anticipating this pedagogical method, the early modern essayist Montaigne expressed his exasperation with a widespread human tendency. "It is a common vice," he writes, "not of the vulgar only but of almost all men, to fix their aim and limit by the ways to which they were born." To combat our credulity, he described his desire to "pile up here some ancient fashions that I have in my memory, some like ours, others different, to the end that we may strengthen and enlighten our judgment by reflection on the continual variation of human things." Montaigne was confident that by "piling up" these examples, he could encourage us to stop thinking parochially and recognize that men and women have lived many different ways according to many different ideals and customs. Unsettled by the diversity, we will be levered away from an atavistic loyalty to our particular way of viewing the world.

But the ancient fashions Montaigne catalogues are not simply diverse. He chooses very carefully, and in a way that anticipates postmodern approaches to history and culture, his examples tend toward the prurient and base. Montaigne quotes ancient descriptions of how people wiped themselves after bowel movements, as well as peculiar postcoital practices. The shock, then, is redoubled, for not only do we see the diversity of cultures, but Montaigne's choice of examples encourages us to worry that those beliefs and practices we were raised to think so decisive for human decency and moral rectitude will come to seem as silly and pointless as the ancient Roman expectation that men should pluck all the hairs off their chest, legs, and arms.

WHAT MONTAIGNE sought to achieve has become the very ideal of what we now call critical thinking. He wants us to soften our loyalty to the immediate and seemingly self-evident truths of our inherited way of life, separating ourselves inwardly from our cultural context. To think responsibly about culture, morality, and religion, in other words, involves removing oneself from the immediacy of conviction, establishing critical distance — a telling metaphor. Just think about modern biblical criticism. In most cases, the basic strategy of instruction is to force pious students to step back from the immediacy of the canonical form of the text and see how what seems to be a doctrinally consistent and spiritually unified whole is, in fact, text made up of heterogeneous sources and layers of editorial revision.

Or, more simply, consider the term "Hebrew Bible," which is now replacing "Old Testament." This terminological shift has many sources, including an anxiety about Christian supersessionism. However, among them is a pedagogical goal. We are told not to engage these ancient writings as elements of a unified witness to the crucified and risen Lord. We are warned against reading the servant songs in Isaiah as pointing toward Christ. Instead, we are told to keep the prophetic power of the text at an arm's length and allow the text to speak to us as a witness to a now dead thing called "Ancient Israelite Religion." This pedagogical strategy distances us and our reading of the Bible from the ferment and fervor of living religious passions — passions that might overwhelm the cool judgment of the historical scholar, passions that we fear will lead to intolerance and religious violence.

I do not wish to issue a blanket condemnation of the pedagogy of critical distance. How can we undertake historical, social, and cultural inquiry without, in some way, breaking the magic charm of immediacy, without stepping back, at least for a moment, from our inherited context and preconceptions? Furthermore, in the Socratic tradition that has exercised such a deep and fruitful influence over the development of Western culture, the leverage of objection and counterargument forces a moment of reflective hesitation that can heighten rather than diminish our ardor for the truth. Reasons against evoke stronger and more profound reasons for. My point, then, is not to criticize the critics. Rather, I want to draw attention to the spiritual consequences of critical distance, consequences that now prevail in spite of the best intentions of scholars and professors.

To learn that Muslims have many wives, that Hindus have many gods, and that Eskimos have many words for snow yields no insight other than the recognition of diversity. The effect is not to shift our loyalty from appearance to reality, as Plato portrayed the effect of the dialectic of Socrates. Nor does cultural study follow the pattern of modern science, where, for example, we move from the illusion of a moving sun that rises at dawn to the accurate knowledge that the earth rotates on its axis. Quite the contrary. The modern critical project has undermined our confidence that any moral or cultural system should properly command our full and uncritical loyalty. As John Henry Newman observed, critical thinking has "a tendency to blunt the practical energy of the mind." It loosens the bonds of commitment and distances us from the immediacy of truths we once thought unquestionable. Critical distance may free us from prejudice, but it also tends to undermine the hope that any enduring truths might be found. It engenders a humility that sustains tolerance, but it can so relax the ardor of the intellect that our civility lacks conviction, and our tolerance becomes indistinguishable from a defeated sense that there are no trustworthy standards by which to judge belief and behavior.

The ways in which these features of modern intellectual life lead to acedia are, I think, obvious. The very sentiments that the classical Christian authors feared are precisely the virtues modern educators seek to instill in their students. The *lento amore,* the slow love that Dante thinks must be purged from our souls, finds approval as the dispassionate heart that establishes critical distance and waits for compelling evidence. The *sterilitas animae* that so worries Bernard of Clairvaux describes quite well the ideal of a critical thinker who has purified himself of the corrupting parochialism that limits his larger, more universal vision. When someone prefaces a comment with the confession that he is speaking, after all, from a "white male, upper-middle class perspective," it reveals either a competition for the upper hand ("I am more critical than you are"), or a despair of ever saying anything either broadly consequential or compellingly true.

CRITICAL DISTANCE is not the only feature of our postmodern context. We can never achieve an entirely carefree approach to life. Yet, the very nobility of our modern moral commitments can create a distance as debilitating as critique. Since no actual society or movement lives up to our ideals, we easily end up unengaged in fact and in action — pushing ourselves away from evil rather than seeking the good. Controlled by what the old writers called *fastidium,* a fastidious conscience, we might boil with outrage on the surface of our souls, while at a deeper level we go slack. Thus, many so-called seekers do not seek at all; they wait for something worthy of their allegiance and the waiting becomes habitual and comfortable. Our society has far more of these "waiters" than "seekers."

This fastidiousness is manifest in our cultural response to suffering, the second feature of our current intellectual and moral landscape that strikes me as emblematic. We recoil from cruelty, and this dominates our collective conscience as the *summum malum,* the greatest evil. Here as well Montaigne anticipates. In his essay "Of Cruelty," he expresses a sentiment now widespread. "Savages do not shock me," Montaigne writes, "as much by roasting and eating the bodies of the dead as do those who torment them and persecute them living." The taboos of traditional morality may loosen their holds over our moral imaginations as we cultivate critical distance, but no pure vacuum develops in their absence. Instead, our sensitivity to suffering and our horror over cruelty increase. If you doubt this trend, just consider my grandmother, who went to a public hanging at a county fair in Hannibal, Missouri, when she was a child. Today, we shudder at the thought. How, we ask ourselves, could our forebears have been so insensitive to suffering and cruelty?

I certainly do not intend a global criticism of our present squeamishness. We should be thankful that *something* of moral significance has filled the void created by critical consciousness. At least we cannot gaze upon torture and suffering with a dispassionate and carefree attitude. Nonetheless, we must recognize how contemporary moral sensibilities tempt us toward acedia.

Detached from the subtle texture of traditional morality, our convictions tend toward vague ideals and general sentiments — "suffering is evil," "all men are equal," "individual freedom must be respected." The impossible universality overwhelms our immediate duties and corrupts our ability to function within the complexities of ordinary moral relations.

Judith Shklar, an astute student of modern political and moral theory, was keenly aware of the demoralizing spiritual consequences of modern liberal ideals, especially the enclosing, immobilizing danger of our heightened sensitivity to suffering. As she wrote, "To hate cruelty more than any other evil involves a radical rejection of both religious and political conventions. It dooms me to a life of skepticism, indecision, disgust, and often misanthropy." Bewitched by abstract ideals, the teacher despairs over the frightfully unequal distribution of talent. The judge anguishes over the need to pronounce painful verdicts. Sensitive solicitude for humanity becomes a threat to moral ideals, and we are tempted toward a compartmentalized mode of thinking. We cherish ideals that operate six feet off the ground, and all the while we live according to a pessimistic and amoral ethic of necessity in the practical affairs of life, an ethic we reluctantly accept and impose.

The misanthropy is usually swaddled in kindness and wrapped in fine moral sentiments, but it manifests the symptoms of acedia nonetheless. How many parents fail to muster the determination to discipline their children because they cannot bear inflicting the suffering it will require? How many educators have resisted the necessity of grading, not out of lassitude or neglect, but because they shrink from the thought of the hurt feelings of those who do poorly? The examples are but instances of a broad cultural trend. Demand and expectation are hurtful; therefore, we turn away from high standards in order to soften the blows of discipline. Our general commitment to reduce suffering causes us to hesitate from inflicting the pain of shame. Acedia, a languid disregard for moral and social standards, has become a virtue.

The evidence is strong. Our present culture of affirmation, self-esteem, and indulgent tolerance is not based on an Emersonian conviction that each person is lit with genius. No, we hold our tongues and smile politely when people tell us of their divorces, abortions, infidelities, and transgressions because we do not want to make anyone feel bad. We indulge and we trim, because the thought of suffering paralyzes. Fixed on the horror of cruelty, the fastidious conscience is brought to inaction by the very passion of its commitment. Fearing evil — why add to the grief of divorce by condemning it? — we withdraw from action.

HOW CAN WE overcome the distances required by critical thought? How can we reenergize the fastidious conscience that cannot countenance the "no" of discipline? How can we avoid the deflating dispassion of a culture preoccupied with the dangers of deeply felt convictions? What are we to do about urgent moral and political causes so broad and unfocused and abstracted from reality that we too easily resign and withdraw? These, to my mind, are among the most crucial spiritual questions we face in our strange, postmodern world.

First, we need to realize that a great deal of modern theology has attempted to turn the afflictions of acedia into signs of virtue. Consider Paul Tillich's formulation of the "Protestant principle." It is the negation of all positive, finite, and worldly forms of faith and practice. In this way, Tillich makes critical distance into a form of faith. "What makes Protestantism Protestant," he writes, "is the fact that it transcends its own religious and confessional character, that it cannot be identified wholly with any of its particular historical forms." The stepping back that marks critical thought is, then, the essence of true religion. "Protestantism," Tillich continues, "has a principle that stands beyond all its realizations." "It is not exhausted by any historical religion; it is not identical with the structure of the Reformation or of early Christianity or even with a religious form at all." Or still again, "The Protestant principle . . . contains the divine and human protest against any absolute claim made for a relative reality." Thus, Tillich draws a conclusion widely repeated in progressive, modern theologies: "Nobody can have the ultimate, nothing conditioned can possess the unconditional. And nobody can localize the divine that transcends space and time." Or to quote from a bumper sticker version of the same: My God is too big to fit into any one religion.

If Tillich's Protestant principle is true, then why in the world would anyone experience, let alone give in to, a burning desire to come to the Lord in baptism and worship? If nothing conditioned can possess the unconditioned, if the finite is not capable of the infinite, then who would not despair of the religious life? Contrary to Tillich, we must stop pretending the distance and dispassion of modern intellectual life are covert forms of faithfulness. Critical thought may produce what Saint Paul, in 2 Corinthians 7, calls worldly grief, the sorrow that any honest person must feel when he recognizes that sickness, disease, and death conquer finite flesh. But we must be crystal clear. Critical thought does not and cannot produce the godly grief that Saint Paul commends. That comes from repentance and personal change, not critical insight.

THIS LEADS ME to my second observation. In Dante's *Purgatorio,* the principle of sacramental penance holds sway. Vices are cured by their contrary, and thus, the slow and tepid love of the slothful is purged by a frenzied fervor. So, in a picturesque scene, just as Dante and Virgil doze off on the ledge of *lento amore,* they are awakened by a crowd of penitents rushing by, shouting and weeping with overwrought passion. "Sharp fervor," says Virgil to those who run by, "makes up for negligence and delay which you showed through lukewarmness in doing good." Here, we need to be careful not to moralize, for according to Dante, as for all premodern writers, the great work of charity is first and foremost the work of prayer. To the extent that we are brought to dispassion by critical thought, we must enter into the disciplines of daily prayer with all the greater fervor and commitment. The more we feel the torpor of critical distance, the more we swiftly must run toward the daily office, toward regular study of scripture, toward the bread and the cup of the Eucharist. An intimacy with divine things provides the reliable way forward to a passion for divine truth. We cannot enjoy that which we hold at a distance.

This insight also holds for the intellectual life. Critical distance easily produces a *torpor animi.* But we must resist the temptation to forever look behind or above or below. At some point, we must train our minds on some aspect of study, whether Wordsworth's *Prelude* or a puzzling question in topology. We must allow ourselves to be romanced and ravished by the promise of truth. As Saint Bonaventure observes in the prologue to the *Itinerarium mentis in Deum,* those who study must be "anointed with the oil of gladness" so that they might be inflamed with desire for wisdom. If we are to fight the noonday devil of acedia, then the *lento amore* of critical distance needs to be counteracted by forms of intellectual life that hasten toward an embrace of truth. Desire for truth and a willingness to risk the soul-engrossing matrimony of conviction must have the upper hand over fear of error.

Evagrius Ponticus offers a different remedy for sloth. For him, the single great weapon against acedia is stability. This seems to contradict Dante's rushing throng, but it does not. The penitent are hurrying away from their negligence. Evagrius, however, is not concerned with how to restore the fallen, but with how to prevent the monk from falling in the first place. He writes, "The time of temptation is not the time to leave one's cell, devising plausible pretexts. Rather, stand there firmly and be patient." When, a few centuries later, Saint Benedict made stability the centerpiece of Western monasticism, he did so for the same reason. A great stratagem of the slothful is to hurry about from place to place to find a more congenial locale for their spiritual projects. The moment a postmodern seeker finds worship somewhat cold, off he goes to another church to try to find more "vitality," or even more likely, he logs onto Amazon.com and orders a book on Buddhist spirituality. We demand immediate results, and should we experience the dryness and tepidness that come from distance and alienation, we counterattack by distancing ourselves still further.

This agitated search for something higher, something more transparent — "the pure gospel" — comes at a great cost. One can no more play games with separation and divorce in marriage and expect to enjoy the fruits of intimacy, than to do so in one's union with the body of Christ. One can no more serve Christ by loyalty to theological abstractions than serve human beings by loyalty to sentience. Only a focused love can overcome distance. After all, Dante's rushing crowds on the ledge of sloth are not going hither and yon. They are all going the same direction — toward Him in whom all will rest.

KNOWING WHETHER to follow Dante's advice and rush toward intimacy or to heed Evagrius and remain in stable loyalty cannot be reduced to a formula or principle. There are no intellectual solutions to spiritual problems. Like each of the seven deadly sins, acedia must be fought with spiritual discipline. Unfortunately, recognizing and accepting the need for inward, soul-shaping discipline is profoundly alien to our culture, not because we have alternatives, but because we entertain the fantasy of life without spiritual demands. This fantasy is the most important legacy of modernity. For the great innovation of modern culture was the promise of progress without spiritual discipline. All we need to do is adopt the experimental method, calculate utility, institute the rule of law, establish democracy, trust the market. In each instance, scientific knowledge, the machinery of proper procedure, the invisible hand of a well-designed process, or some other bloodless mechanism will carry us forward. If we will but believe in this promise, we are told, then we will be free to neglect our souls. For according to this modern dream, our virtues and vices are inconsequential matters of private taste and personal judgment. Thus, although our society is increasingly willing to use economic incentives and legal sanctions to influence behavior (welfare reform and laws against smoking are signal examples), we insist that all discipline must remain on the surfaces of life. Once economic and legal requirements are met, we insist upon our right to live as we wish.

This fantasy of life without spiritual demands demonstrates the depth of our captivity to acedia. Pride has no role here, for even a self-regarding ambition imposes a certain kind of discipline that shapes the soul. One cannot become a Master of the Universe without focused and determined effort. Our dominant postmodern ideal, by contrast, positively endorses shapelessness. We want to be free . . . to be ourselves. The goal is a tautology, one empty of any will to shape or sharpen our lives. Even as we sculpt our bodies in the gym, we cultivate a languid spiritual disposition, one aptly described by Chaucer:

> For ye be lyke the sweynte cate
> That wolde have fissh, but wostow what?
> He wolde nothing wete his clowes.

In our sloth, we will not wet our feet in the frightening water of any spiritual discipline, Christian or otherwise. For fear of wounding fragile, sensitive egos, for fear of fueling ethnocentric dogmatism, we abandon discipline, or we individualize discipline to the point that it is not discipline at all.

We must wet our claws. Neither Dante's urgent rush toward the truth, nor Evagrius's patient stability, will lead to an exhausted or desiccated existence. On the contrary, the spiritual disciplines they urge serve the end of enlivening intimacy. Their strategies awaken and tether, energize and focus. They wish us to become persons with distinct outlines and deep purposes. Only as such persons can we be partners in fellowship — with the truths we seek and with each other. One can no more desire the blessings of marriage with indifference or a wandering eye, than seek a lasting truth with languid disregard or lack of concentration. This holds true in our relation to God. We must desire holiness and allow the burning coal to touch our lips, and we must be attentive and focused in order to hear the still small voice. We should rush toward our Lord, for we can never become too intimate, and we should wait patiently with him, for he always has something more to give us. To do so, we must place the pedagogy of critical distance and the dictates of conscience within a larger vision of our journey toward the truth, a journey in which the warm and enduring and joyfully constraining embrace of love is to be cherished rather than critiqued, sought rather than feared.

Faith in the Flesh

That Saturday morning in January, I watch as the miraculous winter sun angles through the high window to break upon my daughter's hair, pulled back in a tight, neat bun. Beside my daughter stands her mother, her grandmother, and her great-grandmother. Three generations of women come to hear a fourth, my daughter Rachel, read from the open Torah scroll at her bat mitzvah.

We rise as the words roll out. *Vay'daber elohim et kol ha-d'varim ha-eileh leimor.* Rachel's shoulders are draped with a shimmering cloth that she has chosen as her prayer shawl. She has a silver pointer the size of a large pen in her hand. She is following the verses as she chants them. I can see her making tiny swirling motions with the pointer as it moves across the lines of Hebrew, tracing in her mind the figures of musical ornament that she has learned for singing this portion of the scriptures. My parents are behind me, along with sisters and brother, nieces and nephews, and row after row of friends who fill the sanctuary.

I do not know Hebrew, but she has been practicing this recitation at home, so I know that we are standing because we have come to Exodus 20:1: "Then God spoke all these words." The words God has spoken, the words my daughter will repeat, are the

Ten Commandments. We stand to receive them as they were received in the wilderness of Sinai, as they have been received by countless generations. So I am standing, but I confess that, as with my ignorance of Hebrew, I have only little grasp of the spiritual meaning of what she is reciting.

When I was thirteen, the age of my daughter, I was confirmed in the Church of the Redeemer in Baltimore, Maryland. I still remember the hands of Bishop Doll on my head as he intoned, "Defend, O Lord, this thy child with thy heavenly grace." And had I been defended? Perhaps not in the way in which Bishop Doll might have hoped. Still, on her bat mitzvah day at Beth El synagogue in Omaha, Nebraska, my daughter speaks the words God has spoken. The scroll lives. *Anokhi adonai elohekha asher hotzeitikha me-eretz mitz'rayim mi-beit avadim. Lo yih'yeh l'kha elohim aherim al panai:* I am the Lord your God, who brought you out of the land of Egypt, out of the house of slavery: you shall have no other gods before me.

Shortly after my confirmation I rushed to my Carthages and their hissing cauldrons of illicit loves. Fantasies of immortality clouded my judgment and stoked my arrogance. I sang hymns to myself, using easy Emersonian commitments as devices for spiritual adventure, savoring what I imagined to be my boldness as a mark of achievement. In the lists of love I sharpened my mind as a warrior might sharpen his sword: to rush the citadels and slay my adversaries. I was eager for the bravery of seeking, but I was untrained and unprepared for finding, or being found. I threw myself into quests without caring for the direction. I conjured grails to which I might pledge myself.

Love may not conquer all, but it has felled many young men. At the very point in my life when faith in Christ started to take root in my heart and mind and I was forced back upon myself, I fell in love with Juliana, a Jewish woman.

Make no mistake. There was nothing about Yale University in 1985 that made such a love difficult or even noteworthy. Our lives as students were full of common experiences and common aspirations, and in that bastion of American liberalism, one could easily imagine a Jew marrying a Christian — after all, religion is a "lifestyle choice," is it not?

No less than Eros, American liberalism has its own power. It is like a cultural neutron bomb: the structures of ethnic and religious culture are left standing, but they are emptied of life. Far more unlikely was a young Republican to marry a women's studies major than a Christian a Jew. No, for us, the complications of love were of the universally personal sort. Both of us were in bondage to a desire that was driving us toward a renunciation of alternate possibilities: I shall be yours and no other's. In our own ways we struggled against the straitjacket, but we failed to escape the limitations of our own love, and we were joyful in our failure.

Lo ta'aseh l'kha fesel: You shall not make for yourself an idol.

After we decided to get married, we visited Rabbi James Ponet at the Yale Hillel. He told Juliana that as one committed to Jewish law he was obligated to tell her that what she wished to do was prohibited by God. "As a man," he said, "I wish you the best of luck."

Jim's response was representative. Most contemporary rabbis live in the same pluralistic world as the rest of us. They accommodate and resist; they exercise pastoral discretion and stand firm where they can. For Jews, intermarriage is an issue of fundamental importance, and as we discovered, there were very few rabbis — even fewer in the 1980s than today — who would marry Jews to Christians. We had no interest in seeking out one of the few, for neither Juliana nor I wished to live our religious lives on the edges of our traditions. Both of us were just beginning to seek the centers, to accept the confines of orthodoxy just as we were accepting the limitations of desire in marriage.

We decided that a neutral, secular wedding between Judaism and Christianity would be the worst possible place to be married, for we had no intention of having a neutral, secular marriage. The door to the synagogue was barred, so my wife put herself and her family where they did not want to be: in front of the altar upon which Christians offer the sacrament of the sacrifice of Christ, surrounded by stained glass windows of Jesus and his disciples. We were pronounced husband and wife in the name of the Father, and of the Son, and of the Holy Spirit. The opposite of pallid neutrality is real possibility of suffering. In the moment she became my wife Juliana endured the first blow of intermarriage.

Lo tissa et shem adonai elohekha la-shav: You shall not take the Name of the Lord your God in vain.

We had no more interest in a neutral child than in a neutral wedding, and we certainly did not want to tear the children in two by pretending that we could raise them as both a Jew and a Christian. I remember the conversation well. "The children will, of course, be raised Jewish," remarked Juliana one day. I looked at her and said with coldness, "What do you mean, raised Jewish? You do not go to synagogue. You do not keep kosher. I'm not going to keep my children from baptism just so that they can be raised as bagels-and-the-*New-York-Times*-on-Saturday-morning Jews. If you become a religious Jew, then I am willing to promise that I will support you in raising the children as religious Jews."

I made a promise I did not think I would need to keep, but I had underestimated my wife, or maybe God. That Saturday she marched down the street to the Hillel *minyan.* She announced that we were buying new plates and would keep a kosher kitchen. She was willing to marry me in a church, but she was not willing to see her children baptized. The first blow had awakened her, and she saw that the way forward in her life with me would require seriousness about what it meant to be a Jew. Now I was to learn what it meant to be a resident alien in my own kitchen, an onlooker and supporter of her determined decision to burrow into the encompassing word of God's commandments.

Zakhor et yom ha-shabbat l-kad'sho: Remember the Sabbath day and keep it holy.

Circumcision is a ruthlessly physical act. Waves of emotion swept over me as my eight-day-old son lay screaming and the rabbi recited the prayers and the doctor wielded his scalpel. My mind was utterly disordered by the visceral reality of the event. But one thought came, and it has so lodged itself in my memory that I am very nearly consumed by it to this day.

It was a thought of self-doubt, a worry about the invisibility of my own faith. How many times had I come to the altar of my church to receive the bread and wine? How many times had I confessed my sins and received absolution? How many children had I seen baptized with water and anointed with oil? I cannot count the times, and in each instance I felt the truth of Jesus' promise: I will be with you until the end of the age. He is with us, in our hearts and on our lips.

So I had come to believe as my own path had paralleled my wife's turn toward deepened immersion in the religious life. And yet, there, in the sterile environment of an outpatient room at the hospital, I watched the circumcision and saw God's word in the flash of the knife marking my son's flesh — so physical, so immediate, so shockingly intimate, so permanent. Christ was in my heart and on my lips, but was I unmarked in my flesh, unchanged in the brute reality of my life?

Kabed et avikha v'et imekha: Honor your father and your mother.

At the circumcision of my son, I felt the blow of intermarriage most fully, and it was more terrible than I could have imagined. It was the blow of judgment on my head. I do not mean guilt about anti-Semitism. For most American Christians, that is an easy guilt to bear, a guilt that makes one feel superior for being self-critical and progressive. No, this was a painful moment of self-recognition, for I now felt a question that I could not answer. Where had God's commandment set *me* apart and marked me as Christ's own? Do we — no, do I — make the commandments of God empty, "spiritual" and pious commitments that the currents of culture erode and obliterate the moment I leave the church?

COMPASSION IS a humane sentiment. To seek justice is a noble goal. "Peace on earth and goodwill toward men" — these were watchwords of the liberal institutions that had educated me, institutions with no particular commitment to Christianity. Haverford College, my undergraduate college before Yale, was a veritable monastery of "care and concern." Yale University was ever eager to strike the poses of social justice.

My daughter, however, could not eat cheeseburgers, and her friends found this remarkable. Her very mouth was trained and set apart, day by day. And me? Jesus teaches that what goes into the mouth is not important. What matters is what comes out. And yet what came out of my mouth seemed so generic, so easily molded into the progressive platitudes of our age.

I was afflicted with a singular worry. Christianity — the faith of my forefathers, the basis of all my efforts to be faithful to God — was my inheritance; was it also the fuel for the neutron bomb of which American liberalism was but the trigger mechanism? Was a Christianity that accommodated interreligious marriage a religion that clothes indifference with the rhetorical dress of inclusion and tolerance?

Lo tir'tzah: You shall not murder.

A number of years ago I decided to participate in a reading group at my wife's synagogue. The rabbi was to lead a discussion of *Halakhic Man* by Joseph B. Soloveitchik. I had never heard of Rabbi Soloveitchik (1903-1993), the great interpreter of Orthodox Judaism and especially of Jewish religious law (halakha), but I got the book and read it. It enthralled me — and not the least because, ironically enough, Soloveitchik's description of the halakhic path of concretion seemed to me a beautiful and poetic evocation of the Christian belief in the incarnation.

"When the Holy One, blessed be He, descended on Mount Sinai," writes Soloveitchik, "He set an eternally binding precedent that it is God who descends to man, not man who ascends to God. When he said to Moses, 'And let them make Me a sanctuary, that I may dwell among them' (Exod. 25:8), He thereby revealed the awesome mystery that God contracts His divine presence in this world." In another place he writes, "Holiness, according to the outlook of Halakhah, denotes the appearance of a mysterious transcendence in the midst of our concrete world, the 'descent' of God, whom no thought can grasp, onto Mount Sinai, the bending down of a hidden and concealed world and lowering it onto the face of reality."

This vision of divine self-lowering and contraction captivated me. "Halakhic man, with his unique mode of understanding, declares: the higher longs and pines for the lower." Yes, I said to myself as I read, a thousand times, yes. My head was spinning with insight into how my wife's attempts to conform to halakhic requirements had been teaching me the truth of Philippians 2:5-8: "Let the same mind be in you that was in Christ Jesus, who, though he was in the form of God, did not regard equality with God as something to be exploited, but emptied himself, taking the form of a slave, being born in human likeness. And being found in human form, he humbled himself and became obedient to the point of death — even death on a cross."

Juliana, I thought, was humbling her spiritual aspirations, even to the point of taking the food that entered her mouth as a matter of spiritual significance. Soloveitchik had drawn my attention to Ecclesiastes 12:11, and the nails that firmly fasten divine wisdom to concrete reality. ("These words of the wise are as goads, and as nails . . . which are given by one shepherd.") She was nailing her spiritual journey to the concrete reality of life. And she was as Saint Paul speaking to me: "Let no one trouble me, for I carry the marks of Jesus branded on my body."

Yet, in these reveries of insight and convergence, the glistening knife of circumcision flashed and the blow was struck again.

Throughout his analysis, Soloveitchik juxtaposes the way of

halakhic concretion with the spiritual quest of those who seek to transcend the world, those who wish to climb the ladder of being and kick it away when they reach the eternal. Soloveitchik sees how this spiritual quest creates a fissure in the religious life, one that turns all thought toward the heavenly while leaving this world to its own devices, creating a sentiment that can baldly and callously say, "Let the dead bury the dead." In a rare moment, he allows himself to address Christianity directly, and reveals his worry about the spiritual consequences of a faith that is interested in circumcising the heart while leaving the body unmarked: "How many noblemen bowed down before the cross in a spirit of abject submission and self-denial, confessed their sins with scalding tears and bitter cries, and in the very same breath, as soon as they left the dim precincts of the cathedral, ordered that innocent people be cruelly slain."

IT WAS a line written in the early 1940s as the Europe from which God had delivered Soloveitchik was consuming his community with a furious fire of murderous desire. How many noblemen indeed? When I read that sentence I was overcome with the failure of Christianity. In the self-complimenting haze of our sin, did we imagine that Christ came to circumcise our hearts, only to leave our bodies free to indulge our lusts for power and domination?

I thought of my daughter and son. Their mother was training their hands not to mix milk with meat so that the will of the Lord might be done, on earth as it is in heaven. Hands so trained, I thought, would not so readily take up the sword to slay the innocent, even if their hearts burned with murderous desire. Their hands were being pierced with the nails of divine intention day after day. And my hands, what of them?

Lo tin'af: You shall not commit adultery.

Recently, my then-denomination, the Episcopal Church, had been in the news. We had ordained a gay bishop whose current partner, ex-wife, and daughter joined in the ceremony of consecration. As a so-called conservative, I was asked to participate in a Canadian radio show to discuss the whole affair with some liberal proponents of the gay bishop's ordination.

The radio host made a good effort to address the issues, but, as with so many media events, we traded sound bites and the segment ended. I left the studio and went out onto the street. In my mind's eye I was seeing my son's circumcision once again. The day was warm, but I felt chilled. Have I been honest with myself about modern Christianity? Not only had my church rejected the need to mark the body with the knife of circumcision; it has rejected the very idea that God's commandments can shape or control how we use our bodies. Nothing needs to be submitted to God other than the fine sentiments of the caring heart.

I despaired of an invisible Christianity. Could this possibly be what Saint Augustine imagined when he wrote, "Love and do what you will"? I recalled Soloveitchik: "A subjective religiosity cannot endure. And all those tendencies to transform the religious act into pure subjectivity, negate all corporeality and all sensation from religious life and admit man into a pure and abstract world, where there is neither eating nor drinking, but religious individuals sitting with their crowns on their heads and enjoying their own inner experiences, their own tempestuous, heaven-storming spirits, their own hidden longings and mysterious yearnings — will in the end prove null and void."

There, on the sidewalk, I offered a prayer of petition to God. You have come to us in the human flesh of the man Jesus of Nazareth, but we have insisted upon seeking to obey you without regard to our flesh. Forgive us, O Lord, for we have rendered your Word null and void.

Lo tig'nov: You shall not steal. *Lo ta'aneh v'rei'akha eid sha'ker:* You shall not bear false witness. *Lo tach'mod:* You shall not covet.

NONE OF these memories is consciously with me as my daughter completes the tenth commandment and we sit down to hear the rest of her recitation of Exodus 20. My daughter is a beautiful, mature, well-spoken young lady. She is slipping from my grasp and into her own adulthood. I am proud of her, and the awe of God's words mingles with my awe of her self-possession. Did I ever really hold her in the first place? From the moment my wife marched off to synagogue that first Saturday to lay the foundations for her daughter, to receive the foundation laid centuries before Rachel was even born, I was already letting her go.

Jesus teaches us that for his sake we must be able to hate our mothers and fathers, brothers and sisters. My daughter loves me very much, but she is very conscious that this day of her bat mitzvah is as a hating of her father. She was bitter about the fact that I could not be with her mother at her side as she entered into an intimate fellowship with God — to be his voice to his people through the reading of Torah. She was angry, and she cried about it in the months of preparation prior to the bat mitzvah, but neither the rabbi, nor her mother, nor I could give her what she wanted.

In fact, I did not want to give her what she wanted, for her desire was that obedience to God would not require the pain of renunciation, would not require the visible marks on our bodies, the visible, public mark of distance between me in the pews and her before the congregation. And now, she is before me. She is being ravished by the concentration necessary to chant the ancient Hebrew. She is being drawn near to God. I can only witness. I cannot be by her side to hold onto the hems of her garments as she rises upward with each flourish of the canticle of recitation.

My daughter is feeling the full blow of intermarriage. Why can't we all go together? Why can't all the people she loves journey toward the Lord, linked arm and arm? Why is God setting a daughter against her father? I know these are her thoughts, and because I love her so much, I feel her anguish as the knife of circumcision cuts into her heart. She is entering into the narrow way of obedience, and, for all the joy of that day and the rapture of her voice, the very voice of the Ten Commandments, I cannot join her.

My absence, which is forced upon her, is marking her. She knows I support her every word with my spirit, even though I can understand none of them. But I cannot support her with my voice in the prayer before the reading. I cannot touch her gently before she reads. God is cutting me away from her as he had cut away my son's foreskin, not to harm or destroy or denigrate, but to sanctify her as a woman called to him as a Jew, a Jew who is set apart from the nations into which at this moment I must, of necessity, recede.

As I recede and she is drawn away, I am basked in light, for she is aglow on this day. Adorned with dawn's dew of adulthood, she is radiant. She is a light to her father. Her voice continues to sing the ancient words. The sun's rays drape and illumine her. Her face shines. Cut away from me, she is turning to take up a pair of tongs. She is pulling out the living coals of the divine word. She is flying toward me. My son, sitting beside me, reaches for my hand. I feel the tears on my cheek, and the liquid fire of her voice touching the lips of my unclean heart. O the depth of the riches and wisdom and knowledge of God!

Out of the Ruins

On a Saturday in mid-September 2004, on the feast day of Saint Robert Bellarmine, I was received into the Catholic Church. I pledged to believe and profess all that the Catholic Church believes, teaches, and proclaims to be revealed by God. The priest anointed me with the oil of confirmation. I exchanged the peace with gathered friends, and, after long months of preparation, I received the body and blood of our Lord Jesus Christ.

The Martyr's Chapel of St. John's Church on the Creighton University campus was not where I had expected to be on that day. A few years before I had written *In the Ruins of the Church,* which was a kind of manifesto against such a move from Canterbury to Rome. That book diagnosed the pathologies of my former denomination, that often smugly self-satisfied member of the liberal Protestant club, the Episcopal Church. Yet I argued with equal vigor that one should stay put and endure the diminishments of Christianity in our time. I claimed that the disordered state of the Episcopal Church had not led me to despair. I criticized the habits of evasion and strategies of escape that seemed to promise refuge in some other church, and I advocated the vocation of dwelling amidst the ruins.

Publication creates accountability. Hearing of my departure

from the Episcopal Church, a close friend wrote a strongly worded letter reminding me of my arguments for staying put. He cited my own words against me. "I reject our desire for a liberating distance," I had written. "Our vocation is to dwell within the ruins of the church," I had said. And again, "We need to see that in Christ we are not called to love strength and power and beauty. Ruins are not unfit for human habitation."

These words, my friend reminded me, had been read and remembered; they had led people to accept ordination or undertake new responsibilities, in the Episcopal Church and in other decaying mainline denominations. Moreover, these ordination vows and new responsibilities naturally created bonds of obligation that now stand in the way of precisely the move I had made. What, my friend wanted to know, had changed since I wrote *In the Ruins of the Church*? Why did I opt for departure rather than staying put? Do I now think that those who continue to fight for orthodoxy in mainline Protestantism are on a fool's errand?

His questions were difficult. What had changed? A few days after my reception into the Catholic Church, a colleague at Creighton who knows my attraction to dogmatic hyperbole took particular pleasure in observing, "My, my, you look ontologically different." Kidding aside, he was certainly right on one level. I had changed. I once tried to forge a vocation of faithfulness as a loyal member of a liberal Protestant denomination. Now I am a member of the Catholic Church. I changed — I *made* a change. As I look back, however, I do not think I changed my mind about theology or ecclesiology or the fate of Christianity in the modern world. I suppose that, in the end, I changed my mind about myself. All the major premises stayed the same, but the minor premises changed, and with them the conclusion.

To a great extent, I would like to think my arguments for staying put were Augustinian. In his *Confessions,* Saint Augustine tells a tale of his search for God. As a young man he went to Carthage much as young men and women go off to college in our time. He tells of his lustful desires, his "filth of concupiscence" and "excessive vanity," but he seems to have been the kind of student most professors would love to have. In what we might call his freshman year he read Cicero's celebration of philosophy, and the effect was immediate. "I longed," he recalls, "for the immortality of wisdom with an incredible ardor in my heart."

When I read his *Confessions* in my own freshman year, I assumed that this great awakening marked the beginning of Saint Augustine's spiritual journey. Of course, there were many byways and dead ends. He fell in with the Manicheans, a heretical group that divided the cosmos into the good, spiritual world of light that battles against the evil, material world of darkness. Worldly ambition and sexual desire deflected him from the true path. Nonetheless, I was convinced that his journey began with his youthful conversion to philosophy. As a young person entertaining his own dreams of deep existential commitments, I presumed that the *Confessions* was all about how Augustine had followed a long and twisting path toward the true answer to perennial religious questions.

WE TEND to see what we want in the books we read. Our culture is one of leave-taking, and it champions the seeker as the hero of the spiritual life. We think we must brave arid deserts and snowy mountain passes in our quest for God. Recall Kierkegaard's leap of faith, William James's will to believe, and Paul Tillich's courage to be. Having read Sartre's hot rhetoric of existential choice and Heidegger's cooler image of the heroic modern man patiently walking the meadows of our disenchanted culture as a shepherd of Being, I came to believe that truth and holiness, like elves and unicorns, had been veiled and hidden in distant realms and secret forests. It was our vocation to energize our souls and get on with the search. Or so I imagined.

After many rereadings of the *Confessions,* I have been mortified to discover that Saint Augustine does not commend the great preoccupation of modern Christianity, the quest for faith. For him, the journey of his young adulthood was a futile circular movement. Imagining himself to be a seeker after God, he was in fact ever returning to himself. What began as a projected heroic journey ended in exhausted despair. Ten years after Cicero had ignited a love of wisdom, Saint Augustine reports, "I had lost all hope of discovering the truth." What seemed like a journey was nothing more than the huffing and puffing of a presumptuous soul that thought it could storm the citadel of God with earnest longing and good intentions. The upshot was paralysis, and, as his story unfolds, Saint Augustine adverts more and more to themes of bondage ("the chain of sexual desire" and "the slavery of worldly affairs"), crushing weight and exhaustion ("the burden of the world weighed me down with a sweet drowsiness"), and the irresolvable conflict of a divided will ("the agony of hesitation"). When one reads what Augustine actually wrote rather than what one imagines he must have written, the warning is clear. What had seemed a great and noble journey — to find God! — was, says Augustine, a series of delays and postponements. He had not struggled across spiritual deserts, nor had he climbed snowy mountain passes. By his own accounting, Augustine had spun endlessly, "turning over and over again," exhausting himself on "the treadmill of habit."

When I finally got my mind around the logic of Augustine's story, I was chastened. We live in a world of spiritual confusion no less disorienting than Saint Augustine's. We certainly have many Carthages hissing with cauldrons of illicit loves. Just flip through the cable channels in the evening. We have Peter Singer at Princeton, a present-day spokesman for our present-day Manicheans and their crazy rationalism. I have been to Boulder, Colorado, and I have visited the shops that sell Tibetan prayer flags and audio CDs that promise to teach us how to achieve wholeness. Even in Omaha, Nebraska, where I live fully surrounded by the great sea of political conservatism, the bookstores are well stocked with light reading for every seeker imaginable. Can we navigate through this riot of spiritual choices? Augustine's story is a warning. Beware launching out on a search for God, for, as Augustine asks, "What am I to myself but a guide to my own self-destruction?"

The flora of the present-day cultural environment is not limited to pre- and post- and non-Christian species. First Presbyterian sits hard by Second Baptist. Saint Leo's Catholic Church is down the street from All Saints' Episcopal. River of Life Community Church has its advertisement in the Saturday paper, along with Pacific Hills Lutheran and Sunny Slope Christian and the Vineyard Church and countless others. What are we to do in this jungle of denominationalism? Can we, sinful men and women that we are, hope to succeed in the project of deciding which churches are best? When church becomes a choice, will we not guide ourselves to our own self-destruction?

No doubt many will object that this is a purely negative reason for staying put; they will say it is a kind of paralysis born out of a pessimistic assumption that our capacities for spiritual discernment are entirely corrupted by original sin. I think of myself as Augustinian, so I affirm (if that is the word) the corruption. Wherever we are — dabbling in New Age spirituality, cultivating a despairing scientific materialism, attending the local Foursquare church — we may become acutely aware of what we are not finding. We can discern at least that much. But we lack the reliable capacity to get up and start walking in the right direction.

Still, our inability is not a condemnation to stasis. There is a journey of faith for Augustine, but the guidance comes from God, not us. Far from finding God, Augustine confesses, "You pierced my heart with the arrow of your love." Indeed, the arrows had been loosed many times, but in his agitated desire to control his own destiny, Augustine had dodged and deflected them. Only after Augustine has recognized the vanity of his own efforts does the arrow of divine love strike its mark. In the chanting voice of the child beyond the walls of Augustine's garden in Milan, God's work finally penetrates and transforms his heart. "The examples given by your servants," Augustine reports, "burnt away and destroyed my heavy sluggishness." Then and only then does his journey begin: to baptism, back to Africa, and to Hippo.

The general principle of Augustine's own self-analysis is clear, and its relevance to the temptation to embark on our own searches for God is direct — even, and perhaps especially, when that search takes us across the strange terrain of denominationalism. "The soul needs to be enlightened," he writes, "by light from outside itself."

For the great Augustinian tradition of Western Christianity, the "outsideness" of divine light has been expressed by the principle of salvation *sola gratia,* salvation by grace alone. The ever-practical Saint Benedict translated this spiritual insight into the vow of stability. The sinful soul will twist and turn to elude God's grasp, and for monks, this is manifest in the all too human tendency to wander from place to place in an effort to find a congenial community and a sympathetic abbot. For Saint Benedict, this tendency is understandable. Who wants to endure the spiritual mediocrity of a less-than-ideal monastery, and who wants to be subjected to a less-than-saintly abbot? Yet, as Saint Benedict realized, what is humanly understandable may be spiritually disastrous. For who shall guide the monk on his spiritual journey from place to place? Whence comes the light that will enlighten the heart of the seeker? Saint Augustine's warning — "What am I to myself but a guide to my own self-destruction?" — was very much on Saint Benedict's mind when he made stability a key element of his rule.

But equally — or perhaps more importantly — Saint Benedict followed Saint Augustine by insisting that the grace of God is real and concrete. The spiritual arrows of divine love take the form of real people, actual texts, and specific institutions, all providentially ordered by God to shape our lives. Grace comes to the monk in the unending round of daily prayer, in the ways in which living in the company of fallen men demands habits of faith, hope, and love, and in the voice of the abbot who, like the Word of God, cannot be avoided. For Saint Benedict, the vow of stability, "staying put," is integral to the training of the soul. One must be still so that the divine surgeon can work his healing art. We cannot embark on journeys to find God, but we can expose ourselves to God. Love is patient, and a love of God cannot be rushing off after clanging bells and clashing cymbals — or finely appointed churches with nice lists of doctrines that one finds agreeable.

Thus, staying put would seem a fundamental spiritual discipline if we are to renounce the fantasy that we are the ones who fashion our identities as followers of Christ. That is the work of the Holy Spirit, not ours. Our job is to be still so that we might be fashioned by grace. T. S. Eliot, an Augustinian Anglican after my own heart, insisted upon the spiritual imperative of stillness in the *Four Quartets.*

> Descend lower, descend only
> Into the world of perpetual solitude,
> World not world, but that which is not world,
> Internal darkness, deprivation
> And destitution of all property,
> Desiccation of the world of sense,
> Evacuation of the world of fancy,
> Inoperancy of the world of spirit;
> This is the one way, and the other
> Is the same, not in movement
> But abstention from movement; while the world moves
> In appetency, on its metalled ways
> Of time past and time future.

I had no intention of retreating into Cistercian silence, but in my argument for staying put, for trying to be a faithful Christian in our strange times without moving about from denomination to denomination, I tried to do justice to the Benedictine application of Saint Augustine's basic insight. We must resist the world's restlessness. We must abstain from its movements so that God might move in us.

AND YET, I have not stayed put. I left the Episcopal Church and joined the Catholic Church. Why? Partly because I realized that I had turned my Augustinianism into an idea, a theory, a theology. But this is obscure, and to explain I must digress into the thought of another apostate Anglican.

John Henry Newman has long been one of my favorite writers. His ability to combine syllogism with sentiment is remarkable, and I have always been romanced by the long, cloistral, silver-veined sentences that give my students fits when I assign him. I fondly recall first reading Newman's *Apologia* in Hans Frei's class on modern theology at Yale Divinity School. Frei was at his twinkle-eyed, mysterious best when he asked us just what we thought of the famous "Note on Liberalism," the appendix in which Newman deliciously translates the antidogmatic spirit of the age he so disliked into eighteen pithy doctrines.

Newman was to me an accelerant. His observation (drawn from his study of the Arian controversy) that "the truth lay, not with the *Via Media*, but with what was called the 'extreme party'" struck me as a bracing correction to the sensible liberalism of my childhood and education. He endorsed the principle of dogma. "Religion as mere sentiment," he wrote with denunciatory directness, "is to me a dream and a mockery." He had no patience with vague, spectral, and all too malleable fantasies of spiritual fellowship. Like Augustine, Newman saw no hope in seeking. The basis of the Christian life is not our longing; it is the "visible Church, with sacraments and rites which are channels of invisible grace." We cannot move through the spiritual life as we drift through the marketplace. Dogma and the sacramental system must define and circumscribe our lives. If I still retained remnants of

Schleiermacher or Tillich (the heroes of my youth), after reading Newman I wished to be rid of them.

Thus, I wrote *In the Ruins of the Church* for a dual purpose. I wanted to advance Newman's criticisms of liberalism, criticisms I took to be aligned with the postliberal theologies of my graduate professors, Hans Frei and George Lindbeck. Yet, precisely because I was convinced as much by Newman's catholicism as by his antiliberalism, I wanted to do so without standing at a distance from my own church. Dogma and the sacramental system are the foundation of life in God. They are his arrows of love. I had to stay put in order to avoid drifting off into the ether of mere sentiment. I had to avoid making an idea or, worse, a theology the basis for my own thought and action. In the end I failed, and I failed in a way that Newman recognized in his own *Apologia.*

Newman is excruciatingly detailed in his account of his own thinking, but for my purposes, I can simply report his conclusion: he came to think that the basic rationale for Anglicanism lacked validity. Even more strongly, he came to think that Anglicanism was a midwife for a liberalism that led to atheism. I still do not think Newman correct in the way he sets up Anglicanism, liberalism, and atheism as falling dominos, but in my own analysis, I certainly came to think that the Episcopal Church was disastrously disordered and disarrayed. My own reasons and my own analysis are of no more moment than Newman's. What matters is the way one responds to the judgment that Anglicanism is in ruins.

In his *Apologia,* as he looks back, Newman reports that the realization that his prior confidence in Anglicanism was mistaken did not produce an immediate conviction that he must leave. He developed a figural interpretation of his circumstances that justified staying put. "I am content," he wrote to a friend at the time, "to be with Moses in the desert, or with Elijah excommunicated from the Temple." When I wrote *In the Ruins of the Church,* I also adopted a figural strategy to make sense of my situation. I clearly saw that the apostolic inheritance bequeathed to the Episcopal

Church — a liturgy more medieval than reformed, a veneration of the ancient creeds, a love of the Church Fathers, a scriptural piety that did not confuse being learned with being critical — was being dismantled by a revisionist ideology that knew no limits. But I did not see myself as a prophet who hectored at a distance. I appealed to the scriptural figure of Nehemiah's return to the ruins of Jerusalem. The gates of the temple had been thrown down, but rather than leave in despair, we should follow Nehemiah's pattern and live in the ruins of the church with redoubled loyalty.

Under the influence of Ephraim Radner, the figure of Nehemiah's return to a destroyed Jerusalem was embedded in a larger, more comprehensive figural interpretation of our situation as late-modern Christians. In his ambitious study of the history of Western Christian theology since the Reformation, *The End of the Church,* Radner places the destiny of the church within the passion of Christ. Like his body crucified and broken, the divided churches in the West are undergoing a paschal suffering. Thus, I thought of staying put as a form of spiritual discipline. If I followed the path of Nehemiah and drew near to the ruins of the church, then I would be closer still to my Lord.

FIGURAL INTERPRETATIONS are not intellectual items that can simply be judged true or false. They are attempts to make sense out of disparate data and experiences according to patterns within scripture, and they either compel us as deep, structuring insights, or they do not. I imagined that Radner's larger figural interpretation of our vocations as modern Christians (and my Nehemiahan figure) had the power to justify and guide an orthodox loyalty to a ruined church. I would not have written *In the Ruins of the Church* had I not believed that the paschal figure of Christ really is present in the increasingly debilitated and diminished forms of apostolic Christianity that one finds in the Episcopal Church, just as Newman would not have remained an Anglican if he had not believed his own figural interpretation of his situation. The problem was not that I had failed to notice that Anglicanism was a mess. Rereading Newman, I discovered that the problem was with myself and the way in which I had come to hold my figural interpretation.

As Newman looks back on his own figural interpretation, he uses some of his most potent swearwords. He calls it "a theory" that fed a "methodistic self-contemplation." Moses in the Sinai desert may be clearly depicted within the biblical text, and it may have a powerful reality in the lives of countless Christians. One thinks of Martin Luther King's own prophetic evocation of Moses the night before his death: he sees the Promised Land but he cannot enter. But in retrospect, Newman recognizes that his own use of the figure lacked reality. It was a theory, an idea, a theological construct designed to fit his circumstances. He used the figures of Moses and Elijah to comfort himself, but they did not structure his sentiments and habits. He had not been, in fact, content in the desert. He could not live in excommunication.

At various points after the election and consecration of Gene Robinson (a man who divorced his wife to live with his male lover) as bishop of New Hampshire, I found my real ability to be loyal to the Episcopal Church slowly evaporating. The indifference to apostolic tradition and constraint overwhelmed me. I may have wanted to return to the ruins of the church with Nehemiah's devotion, but in reality I was thinking bitter thoughts as I sat in my pew. The most innocuous little divergences from the Prayer Book made me angry. The sermons of my quite faithful rector were subjected to an uncharitable scrutiny. I made caricatures of church leaders and engaged them in tiresome imaginary debates. The good people of my parish lost their individuality and were absorbed into my mental picture of "Episcopalians," people to whom I would be heroically but lovelessly loyal.

The whole point of my figural interpretation of loyalty to the fallen stones of Jerusalem was to follow Christ, who so loved our destroyed world that he died for us on the cross. He did not kick the dust off his feet and leave the earthly city that rejected him. When I wrote *In the Ruins of the Church,* that figure seemed to have a real existence for me. "Yes," I said to myself, "I must follow the way of the cross and stay put." Perhaps I was only deceiving myself then. I am not entirely sure, but I am sure that in 2003 the figure had lost its hold on my sentiments and habits. It had become (to use Newman's epithet) a theory. Nehemiah, who goes with Christlike love to a ruined Jerusalem, may have lived on in my mind, but my spirit was overtaken by a waspish bitterness that contradicted in my life what I had tried to argue in my book.

Modern Christianity is modern precisely in its great desire to compensate for what it imagines to be the superannuation, impotence, and failures of apostolic Christianity with a new and improved idea, theory, or theology. The disaster is not the improving impulse. I certainly wish that all Christians would hope for better from their teachers and leaders. The problem is the source of the desired improvement. For Newman, "theory" is a swearword because it connotes the ephemera of mental life, ephemera easily manipulated according to fantasy and convenience. Yet, in my increasing disgruntlement, there I was, more loyal to my idea of staying put than to the actual place that demanded my loyalty. It was an artifact of my mind that compelled me to stay put. Unable to love the ruins of the Episcopal Church, I was forced to love my *idea* of loving the ruins. With this idea I tried to improve myself, after the fashion of a modern theologian.

Modern theology is profoundly corruptive. The light of Christ must come from outside, through the concrete reality of the scriptures as embodied in the life of the church. The whole point of staying put is to resist the temptation to wander in the invented world of our spiritual imaginings. Saint Augustine wandered thus, and as he reports, the motion was circular and futile. Now my real loyalty to the flesh and blood of an actual, existing church was evaporating, and I was in danger of trying to navigate by my own ideas. My situation was all the more dangerous because my ideas had the tone and tenor of good old-fashioned Augustinianism.

"I will obey my faithless abbot," I insisted to myself. "Why?" I asked. "Because my theory requires it," I replied. "But then to what am I loyal — to my theory or to what God is telling me in the strange instrument of an increasingly apostate church?" By spring of 2004 the answer was clear. I was loyal only to my theory. The words of Saint Augustine haunted me: "What am I to myself but a guide to my own self-destruction?"

I CANNOT SAY whether mainline Protestantism's ongoing dalliance with apostasy prevents any particular man or woman from living in a substantial loyalty to the primary instruments of grace that endure within a mainline church. I have friends whose commitments to staying put are real and not theoretical. They are an inspiration to me. The faithful Episcopalian and Lutheran and Methodist who can be still and stay put out of love for the fragments of the apostolic tradition that continue to be radiant with divine love are exhibiting, I think, an enviable spiritual discipline. Moreover, the support they provide to mainline Protestantism is of incalculable value, not only to their communities but also to the strange and vulnerable ecosystem of American Christianity.

I had hoped to provide my friends with the support of companionship in loyalty to a ruined church, but my errand became spiritually foolish. I turned staying put into a spectral idea that took the place of a living reality. I turned it into a theory of self-appointed spiritual heroism that was neither spiritual (for it was laced with bitter anger) nor heroic (for it was notional rather than real). I perverted Ephraim Radner's scriptural figure, because in the corruption of my heart I made it empty and void.

In the end, my decision to leave the Episcopal Church did not happen because I had changed my mind about any particular point of theology or ecclesiology. Nor did it represent a sudden realization that the arguments for staying put are specious. What changed was the way in which I had come to hold my ideas and use my arguments. As my interior life was becoming more and more alienated from the concrete reality of the Episcopal Church, I was becoming increasingly dependent upon my theory of loyalty. In order to escape the insanity of my slide into self-guidance, I put myself up for reception into the Catholic Church as one might put oneself up for adoption. A man can no more guide his spiritual life by his ideas than a child might raise himself on the strength of his native potential.

STORIES OF CONVERSION to the Catholic Church can be rather tediously joyous. One might wish for some variety in such stories, perhaps something along the lines of Winston Churchill's observation that "democracy is the worst form of government except for all those other forms that have been tried from time to time." But such variety as there is in conversion stories would seem to rest in the different ways in which converts describe a newly found bounty. For me, the gain was fairly simple.

The Catholic Church did not deliver me from apostasy and false teaching. I teach at a Jesuit University, so I am not naive about just how insouciant about orthodoxy priests can be. Nor did Catholicism provide me with a neat, efficient, and trouble-free church. I do read newspapers. What my reception into the Catholic Church provided was deliverance from the temptation to navigate by the compass of a theory. The Catholic Church has countless failures, but of this I am certain: Catholic Christianity does not need to be underwritten by an idea.

A Pentecostal friend came to the mass of reception at the Jesuit Martyr's Chapel. He is a close friend and a man whose faith I admire. After the mass we talked for a while. He asked me, "So, what did it feel like to become a Catholic?" I told him, "It felt like being submerged into the ocean." He reacted with a look of thinly disguised horror. That look reminded me that, while I sometimes suffer from an attraction to Emersonian fantasies of self-reliance and disdain for hierarchy, I had never wanted to be alone with God. It has always seemed to me that such a desire too easily turns into a longing to be alone with one's idea of God, and that is the same as being alone with oneself.

The ocean needs no justification. It needs no theory to support the movement of its tides. In the end, as an Episcopalian I needed a theory to stay put, and I came to realize that a theory is a thin thread easily broken. The Catholic Church needs no theories. She is the mother of theologies; she does not need to be propped up by theologies. As Newman put it in one of his Anglican essays, "the Church of Rome preoccupies the ground." She is a given, a primary substance within the economy of denominationalism. One could rightly say that I became a Catholic by default, and that possibility is the simple gift I received from the Catholic Church. *Mater ecclesia,* she needed neither reasons, nor theories, nor ideas from me.

The End of the Road

The road dominates the American imagination, from the Oregon Trail to Route 66. Behind the wheel everyday life fades into the background. Radio cranked up, rolling wheels gobbling up the miles, corn rows a blur, a big western sky opening out in front — the road trip remains a lasting romance, an image of that strange in-between time of escape, freedom, and adventure. Still, I was surprised to learn that my daughter had been assigned *On the Road* in her high school English class. Kerouac's frenetic novel of careening characters seemed less obvious a choice than *Moby Dick* and less safe a choice than *To Kill a Mockingbird.*

But I soon discovered that my daughter's assignment reflects an emerging consensus about American literature. The Library of America series put out a Kerouac volume in 2007 to mark the fiftieth anniversary of the publication of *On the Road.* A number of other books devoted to Kerouac and *On the Road* hit the shelves of the big bookstore chains. Literary journals published retrospectives. These signs point to a remarkable fact: Jack Kerouac's evocation of the ragtag beatnik culture of his day has entered the canon of Great American Novels. After rereading the novel, I found myself surprised by my own critical assent.

On the Road is a thinly fictionalized account of Kerouac's road trips in the late 1940s. A talented working-class kid from Lowell, Massachusetts, Kerouac was recruited to play football at Columbia University in 1941. After two years he dropped out to become a writer, living in New York City as the proverbial struggling artist.

It was there that he met Allen Ginsberg, William S. Burroughs, and other poets, writers, and wandering souls. Kerouac dubbed his little group the Beats. The name came from a street slang term for down and out, but, when applied to the literary crowd, it was meant to capture the ragged, free-spirited existence of those who live on the edges of society. After the traumas of the Great Depression and World War II, the vast majority of Americans eagerly returned to the relative stability of middle-class life, now reaching outward to the newly emerging suburbs. The Beats were the first wave of rebellion against this larger trend. They self-consciously set themselves against the postwar push toward normalcy by surviving on odd jobs, G.I. Bill benefits, and the kindness of friends and family.

On the Road opens in this New York scene of aspiring poets, writers, and seekers. The narrator, Sal Paradise, is trying to make his way as a young writer. But life has become suffused with the "feeling that everything was dead." (In real life, Kerouac's father died in 1946.) The young would-be sages have reached various dead ends. "All my New York friends," Sal reports, "were in the negative, nightmare position of putting down society and giving their tired bookish or political or psychoanalytical reasons."

But a new possibility appears when there arrives in town a man named Dean Moriarty — based on Neal Cassady, a charismatic personality of great importance in the history of the Beats. Abandoned child of a drunk in Denver, sometime resident of reform schools, and con man, Dean is a man of unaccountable energies and appetites. The incarnation of pure American freedom, he casts his spell over Sal's circle of friends. His zest for life galvanizes the seeking literary types living in dank walk-ups in Manhattan. But Dean leaves, and in leaving, he becomes the lure that draws Sal out of New York and onto the road.

The body of the novel is divided into four main road trips, three crossing and recrossing the United States, and the fourth from Denver down to Mexico City. Sal narrates his adventures in the fast-paced fashion of *this happened* and then *that happened.* He meets oddball characters. There are numerous stops and side adventures. And yet, in the blur of events, the story comes quickly to focus on Dean. No matter where the road leads, it inevitably involves finding Dean, being found by Dean, launching out on cross-country drives with Dean, partying all night with Dean, and finally, in Mexico City, being abandoned by Dean.

Kerouac is not subtle about Dean's role. Although Dean steals without hesitation, cheats on his women, ignores his children, and abandons Sal when he is sick, Dean has "the tremendous energy of a new kind of American saint." "Behind him charred ruins smoked," the narrator tells the reader, but Dean rises out of the chaos he creates with a "ragged W. C. Fields saintliness." Soaked in sweat, muddy, and reeking of urine, Dean radiates "the purity of the road." Despite Dean's erratic, destructive, and selfish behavior, Kerouac describes his achievement with clarity: "Bitterness, recriminations, advice, morality, sadness — everything was behind him, and ahead of him was the ragged and ecstatic joy of pure being." The quintessential free spirit, he has the power to turn his back on all the hindering limitations that ordinary folks feel so acutely, the most limiting of which are moral conventions. "The thing," he preaches, "is not to get hung up." But more eloquent than his preachments are Dean's actions.

As Kerouac tells us in a moment of revelation, "I suddenly realized that Dean, by virtue of his enormous series of sins, was becoming the Idiot, the Imbecile, the Saint." The rhetoric of holiness so closely combined with sordid behavior can outrage the pious reader of *On the Road,* but it should not surprise. Kerouac is following a long literary tradition of juxtaposing high and low, sacred and profane, noble and base. Sal writes in order to convey his "reverent mad feelings." Dean is angelic in his "rages and furies," and Sal records that, in a night of revelry, "Dean became frantically and demonically and seraphically drunk." Dean is a con man and a wise man, a mystical lecher, a debauched embodiment of spiritual purity.

THE PROBLEM of happiness is at once social and existential. As Jean-Jacques Rousseau observed early in the modern era, social expectations alienate. The examples are many. Good manners dictate saying "thank you" even when we are not truly grateful. Prudence and anxiety about the dire consequences of poverty encourage us to save for the future and resist the temptation to spend for the pleasures of the moment. Conventional morality condemns as sinful the sorts of liaisons that flow directly from the immediate, unhindered sexual desires of men and women. In each case, and in countless others, what we think and feel and want are at odds with what is expected.

Rousseau was a complicated thinker. His theory of the social contract can give the impression that he endorses the classical picture of happiness as socialization into a community of virtue. But in his influential dramatizations of the good life, *Emile* and *La Nouvelle Héloïse,* he outlined a new approach. Those who wish to live well must break the charm of social conventions so that they can live according to their truest impulses and innermost desires.

The bohemians followed Rousseau's advice in nineteenth-century Paris. Henry David Thoreau and Walt Whitman were New World bohemians, and in the twentieth century the tenements of Greenwich Village became an important center of American bohemian life. The personalities, motivations, and literary movements were different in each case, but they all viewed the rigid social and moral conventions of respectable society as impoverishing and unnecessary.

Rousseau's counsel and the bohemian approach to life can seem an easy hedonism, but it never has been, or at least never merely. Rousseau knew that man is a social animal. We are hardwired to want to live in accord with social conventions. As a result, any sort of deviance that is intentional rather than pathological has a heroic magnificence — a status Rousseau proudly assigned to himself. Not surprisingly, then, one of the defining features of the bohemian project has been a celebration of transgression for its own sake. Those who break the rules — whether artistic, literary, or moral — gain the most admiration, because they have demonstrated their self-willed freedom from society.

The Beats were quintessential bohemians. Kerouac and Ginsberg and the others felt the plain-Jane expectations of middle-class American life as an infecting, constraining force. Wife, career, mortgage, children, savings accounts, quiet suburban streets: these were realities overlaid by the deadening expectations of conventional morality, or at least so thought the Beats. Escape was essential, and although Kerouac and the other Beats lacked Rousseau's clarity about the constant impulse of human nature to accept and submit to social authority, they intuitively recognized the need for dramatic acts and symbols of transgression.

This urgent desire to break free from the penetrating power of society and its ability to define one's life gives an atmosphere of excitement and existential drama to *On the Road,* and makes it wrong to read the novel as a hedonistic story of adolescent self-indulgence and thrill seeking. Just as Saint Francis tore off his clothes in the city square and rejected life according to normal hopes and fears, so Dean is a man entirely outside society. His criminality is not motivated by a mean desire for money. He does not steal cars to sell them, for that would simply be a dishonest way of getting the equivalent of a regular paycheck. Dean commits crimes because it is in his nature to grab whatever is at hand to enjoy the moment. His transgressions, Kerouac tells us, were all part of "a wild yea-saying overburst of American Joy." Dean wants to live, and, as Jesus advises, he cares not about the morrow — while he pops pills, smokes joints, and downs shots of whiskey.

In his conscienceless carelessness, Dean is angelic. "He was BEAT — the root, the soul of Beatific." Dean lives in the moment, one tap of the cymbal at a time.

IN 1957, the *New York Times* review hailed the novel's publication as "a historic occasion." The review trumpeted that *On the Road* offers "the clearest and most important utterance yet made by the generation Kerouac himself named years ago as 'beat,' and whose principal avatar he is." Of course, as David Brooks so cleverly observed in *Bobos in Paradise,* we're all weekend beatniks now. The counterculture of transgression that dominates *On the Road* has thoroughly colonized our middle-class world.

Transgression and marginality have become the new normalcy. The bohemian rejection of social convention was first theorized as a normal stage of psychological development ("adolescent rebellion"), and more recently it has been made into both commercial fashions and academic dogma. Aging rock musicians go on tours and play their songs of youthful lust and rebellion to graying Baby Boomers who need Viagra. College professors theorize transgression as an act of political freedom. It's easy to see that Kerouac's road led from the Beat fantasies of the primal innocence on the margins to the New Left's infatuations with the criminal (Norman Mailer) and the insane (Ken Kesey), and then onward to our own day, where white boys in the suburbs dress like drug dealers, girls like prostitutes, and millionaires like dockworkers. Crotch-grabbing rap singers play the role of well-paid Dean Moriartys.

Perhaps that's why some critics think of *On the Road* as little more than early propaganda for our current culture. Writing in the *New Criterion,* Anthony Daniels argues that Kerouac "was a harbinger" of an age "in which every intelligent person was expected, and came himself to expect, to forge his own soul unguided by the wisdom of his ancestors." We only care about Kerouac, Daniels claims, "because he was a prophet of immaturity." "To call Kerouac's writing mediocre is to do it too much honor," Daniels adds. The book's significance "is sociological rather than literary." And with a *hauteur* one expects from the *New Criterion,* he concludes, "The fact that his work is now being subjected to near-biblical levels of reverential scholarship is a sign of very debased literary and academic standards."

I don't dispute the fact that Kerouac's accounts of beatnik life inspired the adolescent rebellion in the 1960s which eventually became the perpetual adolescence of our own times. But Daniels falls into the usual misinterpretation of *On the Road,* one perpetuated by decades of idealistic, dreamy young readers whom he finds regrettably immature. As a result, he is wrong, both about what the novel says culturally and about what it achieves as a work of literature.

Kerouac was not a writer who anticipated the 1960s, which, in fact, he disliked and denounced before his premature death in 1969. In *On the Road* he does not treat the adventures of the road as a path into the supposedly real self, nor does it lead toward thoughts of a better society. The novel disparages "the complacent Reichiananlyzed ecstasy" of progressive folks in San Francisco. It expresses no confidence that heroin or marijuana or whiskey will bring us to some hidden truth about our souls. The novel is noticeably disinterested in social or economic utopias. There are no communes, no health-food cooperatives, no late-night meetings to talk about revolution.

On the contrary, in *On the Road* Kerouac focuses on the disordered, episodic, and chaotic nature of his experiences. He seems less a prophet of any particular way of life than an observer of the inconclusive thrusts of bohemian desire for authentic life — and the counterthrusts of reality. Sal despairs of "the senseless nightmare road." Faced with embittered friends, Sal tells us, "I forgave everybody, I gave up, I got drunk." The sentiment is resignation, not sybaritic self-indulgence. "Everything," Sal recalls, "was collapsing" as Dean's aimless antics lead to a dead end. Sal follows

Dean, but the promises of the moment seem always broken soon after they are made. While traveling, Sal recalls a lonely song with a telling refrain: "Home I'll never be."

Kerouac's ambivalence is not just a matter of clashing emotions that come from the highs and lows of life on the road. The book is forever careening forward, and the story never rests in any particular observation or experience. Kerouac lists the towns that Dean drives through at high speeds — Manteca, Modesto, Merced, Madera, Pueblo, Walsenburg, Trinidad: transition and movement agitate the novel, and the reader.

Kerouac's accounts of his experiences are either catalogues of indigestible detail or surreal sketches. On one page Sal is drunk in a San Francisco restaurant. A page or two later he is on a bus where he meets a Mexican girl and falls in love. Only a few pages further on he abandons her to make his way back to New York. The novel does not develop. It tumbles. The rat-tat-tat of narration, the quick snapshots of local color, and the raw emotions recalled give the story a feeling of restless seeking rather than sustained introspection, philosophical coherence, or careful social analysis.

This overall literary effect was not accidental. Kerouac took his trips with the self-conscious goal of gathering material for a novel. For a couple of years he struggled with numerous drafts, always unsatisfied with the results. In April 1951, Kerouac decided to begin again. This time he taped together several twelve-foot-long sheets of tracing paper, trimmed to fit into his typewriter as a continuous roll. In three weeks he typed the entire story from beginning to end as one long paragraph on the single scroll of paper.

The marathon performance became something of a legend, and it was romanticized by Kerouac himself as part of his later theory of "spontaneous writing." However, the approach was not a cheap publicity stunt. As Louis Menand has observed, the taped-together sheets of paper constrained and disciplined Kerouac.

The scroll prevented the sort of deepening of theme, character, motive, and experience that comes with circling back to revise. Kerouac did revise later, but mainly to consolidate and simplify the various road trips into a more manageable form. He did not introduce layers of authorial reflection into the relentless flow of events and personalities.

As a result, *On the Road* does not emerge as a bohemian manifesto with a clear agenda or as an existentially deep reflection on the inner life of a countercultural hero. The Beat lingo is omnipresent, and its slogans, aspirations, and hopes are plainly in view. Dean Moriarty is certainly a high priest of transgression. But because these and all the other elements of the narrative cascade through the pages, nothing stands out to sum up or interpret events. The details — and especially the dated existentialist slogans and Beat truisms — fall away because they fall behind. Prose racing forward, the road simply becomes a desperate, necessary, ancient quest for what Kerouac describes in a number of places as "the pearl."

THAT FEELING — of straining, desperate, and failed seeking — does not define the world we live in today. Our tattooed adolescents enjoy small pleasures of rebellion and collect the socially approved badges of nonconformity, all the while presuming nonjudgmental acceptance. Our literature is dominated by the languid Iowa Writers Workshop style: carefully wrought set pieces to accompany our studied and carefully constructed self-images. *On the Road* may have given us our clichés about authenticity, but not our quiescence, not our postmodern roles as managers of difference, not the temperate transgressions that we insist upon as our right as middle-class Americans.

The self-congratulation of the 1960s is entirely absent from *On the Road.* Kerouac does not compliment himself as a rebel after the fashion of Hunter S. Thompson. He is no Hugh Hefner posing as a heroic hedonist. Many scenes are debauched, but Kerouac does not tot up his demerits, like a high school boy bragging about how many beers he drank on Friday night. The book expresses hunger and never satisfaction, not even in its own countercultural image. "I had nothing to offer anyone," Kerouac writes in a line that sums up the effect of the whole book, "but my own confusion."

There is, however, an unexpected, subtle relevance, one that testifies to Kerouac's achievement as a writer rather than his influence as a legendary member of the Beat generation. Sal consistently conveys notes of sadness that grow ever more palpable as the book draws to an end. One drunken episode brings not good times but instead memories of an earlier urine-soaked and unconscious night on the floor of a men's room. The road of transgressive freedom seems haunted by defilement. Sal's final visions in Mexico City do not come from any high at all, but instead from fever-induced delusions as Dean leaves him. Sickness and abandonment take the place of the promised adventure and fellowship of the road.

Most poignantly of all, the novel opens with voluble talk about Nietzsche and Schopenhauer and Proust, but it concludes with Dean's strange, incoherent effusions. By the end, Sal tells us, "He couldn't talk any more. He hopped and laughed, he stuttered and fluttered his hands and said, 'Ah — aha — you must hear.' We listened, all ears. But he forgot what he wanted to say." Dean's mind is so fried by drugs and alcohol that he can no longer carry on a conversation. The seraphic mystic of "pure love" becomes a mute oracle. The great bohemian guru can no longer offer guidance. One feels the need for the road in Kerouac's forward-leaning prose. But the reader also feels the failure. "I think of Dean Moriarty," Sal the narrator writes in his final line, "I even think of Old Dean Moriarty the father we never found." Then, as if wishing to ward off the demons of emptiness and loss, Sal repeats, "I think of Dean Moriarty."

The sad sense of failure and decay in *On the Road* strikes me as far more contemporary than the revelry and debauchery of the novel. We have not inherited Dean's "wild yea-saying overburst of American joy," nor have we found our way to the "joy of pure being." True enough, we smile and congratulate ourselves for our progressive attitudes as we accommodate ourselves to a society committed to embracing any number of strange "lifestyle choices." But, on the whole, our culture seems dominated by worries. The media lust for bad tidings, as if to insist that we must suffer for failing to find the pearl of great price. At elite universities, one can be forgiven for concluding that our academic leaders believe that Western culture does not deserve to thrive, or even to survive — a thought held even as they ride along the surfaces of a remarkable contemporary social tolerance, born of our tacit collective affirmation of the transgressive beatitude of Dean Moriarty.

It is as if we very much want to believe in Dean, but, like Sal at the end of *On the Road,* we know that we cannot rely on him to give us guidance. We want to believe the promises of bohemian life — to live according to our own innermost selves — but we are surrounded by the sadness of disappointed hope. The transgressive heroism of our imagination now looks as tawdry as daytime television. Bohemianism becomes banal and disappointing as it becomes dominant. We suffer the failures of the countercultural project even as we surround ourselves with its music, its rhetorical postures, and its fashions.

I DO NOT claim that Jack Kerouac was a great writer. His later novels are often preachy and lachrymose. But Kerouac's lasting achievement in *On the Road* is beyond doubt. The manic, forward-leaning rush of Kerouac's prose drives his writerly ego to the margins of the narrative. This allows Kerouac to depict the bohemian project rather than offer a statement of its goals or summary of its philosophy or airbrushed picture of its heroism. Kerouac was a witness to the Beat generation, not its poet or spokesman or philosopher king.

It is stultifying to approach literature always expecting moral instruction in the form of ready and true principles for how to live. And it is absurd to reject Kerouac simply on the grounds that he fails to teach sound morals. By all means read Jane Austen. But literature can instruct in many different ways. It can show us how and where the reality of our lives — the urgency of our loves and the aching hunger of our needs — overfloods what we imagine to be our settled and satisfactory views of what makes life worth living.

And when it does, readers are left alone to navigate on their own — to test, as it were, the sufficiency of their own moral resources, to see if cherished ideas can make sense of the strange, pulsing, living, and almost always perverted and confused realities of human life.

So it was for me the first time I read *On the Road* as a college student. A bohemian fellow traveler of sorts, I had already been on my own road, hitchhiking many times across America. The book had a paradoxically sobering effect as I read it one day on the front porch of a hostel in France, outside of Chamonix, overlooking a meadow in late spring bloom. When I finished I felt a judgment on my Emersonian fantasies of originality and existential adventure. My small efforts to escape from the safe streets and calm kitchens of middle-class America were, I learned, part of an old story. I was going down an often-walked road with my emblematic backpack and blue jeans and torn T-shirt. I felt like a suburban explorer who suddenly realizes that the nearby forest is not the Amazonian jungle.

More deeply and more slowly and more unconsciously I also felt the sadness: the incoherent babbling of Dean Moriarty, the sulfurous red dawns that always seemed to follow the all-night reveries, the way in which what Sal wanted seemed to slip from his hands, the mute indifference of the great American landscape that Kerouac evokes so passionately, the hard asphalt of the road itself.

The manic rush of Kerouac's prose lays bare his own ambivalence and self-contradiction. He did not package the bohemian experience with a peace symbol and the earnest pose of a young revolutionary of high moral purpose. He told a story that forced me to consult my own moral compass. He helped me see that Dean Moriarty, the antinomian shaman of the American imagination, achieves no beatitude and has no blessings to give.

Roughnecking It

The beer was thin and tepid. I'm not sure what brand I was drinking, but it really didn't matter much. In 1980 Coors was the outer edge of exotic, and beer ran from pale to paler. Bruce had drifted over to the other side of the loud, crowded barroom. I caught his eye and motioned to see if he wanted another one. He smiled and shook his head no. I scanned the room for signs of Bob, but he was nowhere to be found. Probably out in the back parking lot smoking pot with somebody. Bob was predictable. I ordered myself another beer.

The Flamingo is a large bar, or at least it was until the oil boom eventually went bust in one of the many downturns that give Wyoming its windswept impermanence. I managed to find a seat at the bar along with the other long-haired and ill-shaven guys wearing Carhartts, the Okie-from-Muskogee-goes-to-Haight-Ashbury look that Willie Nelson perfected. The place buzzed while a less than professional band did covers of Marshall Tucker and Lynyrd Skynyrd.

It was a Friday, maybe a Saturday night. I had been working on an oil rig outside of Rawlins for three months. The gas crisis of the '70s had triggered a boom in domestic oil exploration, and I was dipping my straw into the surging current of cash that had brought nearly all the men in the Flamingo that night — and it was pretty much all men — to Wyoming.

Behind me guys pressed forward for drinks. It felt good to swim in the swift and raw currents of a workingman's world flooded with money. I remembered getting my first paycheck on a late Friday afternoon. The drilling rig was more than an hour from town, and all the banks were closed by the time we'd returned. But my boss reassured me that I could go to any bar and cash an oil-field check. So late the next morning I did. The manager told me that he had to charge one dollar per hundred cashed. I assented, and he counted out ten $100 bills and some tens and singles. It was the first time in my life that I had ever held a $100 bill.

Weeks rolled by and paychecks were cashed, and on that night in the Flamingo I was feeling flush and complacent. I was an oil-field roughneck out with his buddies. The place was filling. Voices were loud and urgent with a weekend lust for good times. Another guy knocked against me as he squeezed his way toward the bar. My beer spilled. A little got on him, and he glowered at me as if it had been my fault. "Sorry," I said, and I ordered another, and one for him as well just to show that I was a good guy. When mine came, I turned the glass slowly round in the small pool of foam that slid down its sides. Vacant in alcoholic relaxation and filled with inward satisfaction that came from my repose in the fraternity of the rigs, I drifted slowly into myself.

I HAD KNOWN nothing of oil rigs and roughnecks as I grew up in Towson, Maryland, a pleasant suburb of Baltimore. Lacrosse stick in my hand from an early age, I never signed up for Little League baseball. I should have gone to play for Princeton or Cornell or Brown, and then on to Salomon Brothers or law school. But I was deflected. By age eighteen, a teenage fascination with rock climbing came to predominate. I think it was one of my sister's friends who gave me the push. "If you want to be a rock climber," he told me, or at least my memory tells me, "you really have to go to Yosemite." In September of 1978, instead of going off to college, I hitchhiked west to Yosemite, the place climbers simply call "the Valley."

A couple of weeks turned into the better part of a year. Eager, I soon became accomplished. Two weeks after arriving I had climbed El Capitan. By the end of the spring, as I piled up ascent after ascent, the small, informal, but rigorously elite group of top climbers quietly inducted me into their company. When the legendary Jim Bridwell came over to my campsite, wanting to know what I thought of this or that move on some particularly intimidating route of his, it was like being touched on the head by the king's sword.

But I was not the typical climbing bum stretching a few bucks to stay for another week. I had arrived in Yosemite with Richard Feynman's *Lectures on Physics* in my backpack, as well as Thomas Mann's *The Magic Mountain.* The force that had pressed me away from the college classroom worked against an equal and opposite pressure. By May I was out of money, and I was dimly aware that I could not hang from rock faces forever.

Three months later, my father dropped me off at Haverford, a wonderful monastery of establishment liberalism that eventually educated me, as it had my father and would my brother and, briefly, one of my sisters. But my soul was divided. I was as much on the rocks as in the classroom, at least in my heart. Even lacrosse, that old passion, and girls, a new, or at least newly requited one, failed to break the spell. And so at the end of the year I asked the dean for a leave of absence.

My parents were not pleased, though they mounted no sustained protests. In late July 1980, when my efforts to find work in Baltimore to finance yet another round of rock-climbing adventure yielded little, I asked a friend to give me a start on my hitchhike west. He dropped me off a few miles out of town on I-70. I had about $500 in my pocket, a plan to go to the Tetons, and a few peanut-butter-and-jelly sandwiches prepared for me by my mom.

My backpack was overloaded with garish red and purple nylon climbing ropes and all the shiny gear that clinks and clanks around climbers as they work their way up the rock. In a series of providentially coordinated rides — twice drivers used their CB radios to arrange seamless transfers at rest areas — I rocketed west toward the mountains. An Army cook on leave picked me up just west of Chicago. He drove eighty miles an hour to get to his girlfriend in Omaha as my mind raced in anticipation of grand ascents. Then, as I stood by I-80 near Grand Island, Nebraska, exhaustion led "The Fat Man" (his very accurate CB handle) to stop and, a hundred or so miles later, turn over to me the wheel of his pickup while he snored the night away and I drove straight through to Rock Springs sustained by his cache of Diet RC Cola.

A couple of rides later, I made it to the American Alpine Club Climber's Ranch in the Tetons less than three days after leaving Baltimore. I couldn't have driven faster on my own. And as a bonus, after the sandwiches ran out, the guys who gave me rides had bought me meals. It troubled them that I was willing to go without food all day long in order to keep my small cash hoard untouched. I spent exactly nothing to travel 2,000 miles.

The good fortune was a harbinger. Rick Lui, who had run the Climber's Ranch in the Tetons for at least a decade, knew my type — eager and poorly financed — and he winked as I slept in the woods on the sly. But a day or two after I got there, Bill Nicholson unexpectedly arrived. I knew Bill from my year in Yosemite. He and I would sit by the campfire and talk about how much we wanted to find our way to the big mountains of Alaska. It's one thing to test oneself on the rock faces in the western sunshine; it's another to make one's way across glaciers and up ice-covered slopes.

We climbed the east face of Teewinot together. Sharing a can of sardines on the summit, with the towering north face of the Grand Teton standing sentinel to the southwest, he turned to me. "Rusty," he said, "we've just got to get up to Canada." Picking the last crumbled sardine carcass out of the mustard sauce, I agreed. The next day, as August began, we were driving over Teton Pass and heading north.

Bill's 1965 VW van strained at 50 miles per hour, and the cream-colored dashboard had no radio. Time and silence made for long conversations. But sharing the cost of gas drained me quickly, and by the end of the month my wallet was empty. I think it was on the plains of Alberta, on the way back south, under a boiling ocean of low hanging clouds that made the endless fields and empty roads seem small and lifeless, that he recommended Rawlins as the place to restore my finances. "Just go to the Ferris Hotel downtown," he told me, "and ask the desk clerk if any of the drilling crews need a hand. The pay is fantastic, and they are always looking for somebody." It seemed impossibly precise and vague at the same time, but since Bill was driving through Rawlins on his way back to Denver, I thought I would give it a shot.

THE FERRIS was an old-style, downtown hotel. A few years ago, when I drove through Rawlins, it was shuttered, like, it seemed, half the town, but even then the Ferris was not exactly flourishing. Built in the 1950s during the uranium- and iron-mining boom, it was far from the interstate exits that have sucked commerce out of the old town centers throughout the West and Midwest. Four or five stories of utilitarian beige brick were topped by an impressive neon sign that depicted a steam shovel and spelled out the hotel's name. The lobby featured linoleum, blonde wood, and formica. The day I walked in, two or three old men were sitting in low, vinyl-covered chairs repaired by clear packing tape, silently reading newspapers and magazines.

I had $10 in my pocket, and I knew absolutely nothing about drilling for oil. And I never had much luck finding jobs. I think I tended to be too ambivalent, unable to project the impression, for example, that I'm unaccountably eager and strikingly qualified to wash dishes or paint houses or be a paralegal. To my amazement, when I asked the woman at the front desk if she knew of a drilling crew that needed a hand, she said, "Yes." She went over to a bulletin board beside the rows of small shelves that contained room keys on rings tagged with duct tape. Carefully removing a torn off edge of paper, she gave it to me without a word. On it was written, in a very uneven cursive, "Chain hand needed. Call Kenny. 544-7182."

I had no idea what chain hand meant. The booming oil fields were always in need of workers, Bill had emphasized, but he hadn't been very specific. As I studied the note, the woman was sizing me up. I was not the first fresh-faced young man that rumors of well-paying work had brought to her front desk, and she drew the accurate conclusion that I was a hopeless tenderfoot. Sensing my paralyzing uncertainty, she put me in motion. "Pay phone's over there," she said, gesturing to her left.

The phone call was brief and to the point. "You got any rig experience?" "No." "None?" "None, sir." Long silence. "You willin' to work hard?" "Yes, sir." Shorter silence, and then a voice, growling in concession to necessity, said: "Be ready at seven tomorrow morning in front of the Ferris."

It did not seem more possible just because it became real. Five minutes in Rawlins and broke, a help-wanted ad of the most informal sort, one very brief phone interview, and next thing I knew I had a job making more money than I could ever have imagined possible. A double shift here and there brought two weeks pay close to $1,500 — a fabulous sum for a twenty-year-old in 1980.

But it wasn't just the money that made the job so remarkable. The oil field managers in their four-wheel-drive Suburbans with the company logo on the side made more money. For that matter, the owner of the Flamingo bar made more money, to say nothing of oil-company shareholders, or Wall Street bankers who brokered investments and traded oil futures, or Saudi princes who engineered the oil crisis of the '70s that stimulated the domestic boom in oil exploration that had drawn me into its frothy Wyoming ventures in the first place.

I was none of these, but it didn't matter, because I very quickly came to glory in my newfound identity. Roughnecks work in small, five-man crews on the front lines of the oil patch. They tend to be a high-spirited group with devil-may-care attitudes. We were the tip of the vast money-making spear. We felt it. The town knew it. An on-again, off-again college kid from a quiet Baltimore suburb, I hadn't ever heard of roughnecks, and I had no experience with any other kind of clubby and self-confident workingman's mentality. But there I was. Pushed off the normal path from home to college to career by a passion for rock climbing, I had accidentally found my way into an elite corps of the industrial revolution.

A DRILLING RIG is a massive platform of machinery that sits about two stories above the ground. The floor of the rig itself is about the size of a living room, flanked at the back by two or three monstrous engines the size of large vans, and fronted by a long metal slide that reaches down to lengths of drilling pipe stored at ground level. Along one side of the rig platform is attached a narrow metal building that looks like a suspended mobile office. With droll self-knowledge, roughnecks call this place of occasional refuge the doghouse. The other side has stairs and catwalks that provide access to a tangle of pipes and pumps. Over the rig floor soars the derrick, a 150-foot superstructure of steel that supports various cranes and pulleys.

The purpose of a drilling rig is to bore a hole in the ground to tap reservoirs of oil below the surface. To do so, machinery is set up to function like a giant power drill, twisting a bit that bores ever more deeply into the earth's crust. The huge engines turn the drilling pipe that runs from the center of the platform down and into the ground.

Things get complicated, however, because the hole being

drilled is very deep. In the first place, all the stuff being ground up by the drill bit, the "tool," needs to come up and out of the hole; otherwise, the tool will seize up in the endlessly pulverized stuff at the bottom of the hole. The bits in ordinary hand drills have a spiraling indentation to guide the wood or metal shavings out of the hole. But this does not work if the hole is deep. So the oil-drilling rig is set up to pump a thick, silicon-conditioned mud down the hollow center of the drill pipe and out through jets in the tool. The mass of pipes and pumps to the side of the drilling rig are devoted to this purpose, and if all functions well, then the pressurized mud brings the tailings up and out of the hole. Roughnecks spend a fair amount of time doing the tedious work of preparing the mud and managing the system that circulates it through the hole. There is no romance in this work.

The depth of the hole creates a further problem. If you need to make a six-inch hole in a piece of wood, then you run out to Home Depot and buy a drill bit long enough to penetrate. But what if you want to drill a ten-foot hole — or a ten-thousand-foot hole? You need to find a way to stop and add extenders as the bit presses downward. On the drilling rig, this is accomplished by fixing the tool to thirty-three-foot sections of drill pipe. Every time the drilling reaches down a full length of pipe, the rig boss, called the driller, stops the spinning table at the center of the rig. The rest of the crew assembles to hoist the next section of pipe up the ramp and add it to the string that reaches down into the hole. Once the new pipe section is attached, the spinning process starts again, and the drilling resumes. It is a moment of genuine urgency and concentration. The cranes go into motion. Engines roar. The roughnecks take their place on the rig floor to manipulate the drill pipe.

BUT IT'S ONLY a moment. The bigger problem with deep drilling is what makes the job of roughneck hard, dirty, dangerous — and heroic. Even though drilling tools cost tens of thousands of dollars because they are tipped with industrial diamonds, they wear out every few days and need to be replaced. Here physics and finances conspire. Getting a tool out of ground when it is 10,000 feet below the surface involves pulling a seemingly endless amount of drill pipe up and out. Piece by piece, the long string needs to be broken apart. The pipe is then set aside to be reassembled as the new tool is sent back down to restart the drilling.

This process of pulling out the tool, replacing it, and then sending it back down the hole is called tripping, as in "taking the tool for a round trip." The trip must be done as quickly as possible, because when the tool is not pushing downward toward its profitable destination, the oil company is still paying thousands of dollars a day to keep the rig on the site and the crew on the job.

The need for rapid replacement of the tool is why the derrick rises up so high. When tripping out of the hole, the roughnecks keep the 33-foot pieces of drill pipe in larger, 100-foot chunks. These longer sections are twisted off the string and leaned against the derrick for efficient reassembly. As the tool comes out, the stack of drill pipe grows. Even from a distance you can tell when a rig is tripping, because a great bulk of recently removed drill pipe fills the otherwise delicate metal superstructure of the derrick. It can take an entire eight-hour shift to pull a couple of miles of drill pipe out of the ground, and another whole shift to put it back in.

When tripping, roughnecks work at a rapid pace. Thousands of pounds of metal equipment are thrown into a carefully choreographed process. The derrick hand takes his place, strapped in 100 feet above the rig floor to manage the tops of the 100-foot lengths. The driller mans the controls along the side of the engines, barking orders and throwing levers that work the various cranes, chains, and machines that manipulate the many tons of drill pipe that need to be taken out and then put back into the hole. The workers — the "motorman," the "chain hand," and the "worm" — stand at the center of the drilling platform, breaking apart joints in the drill pipe on the way out and remaking them on the way back in.

The drill pipe is joined together when the male end of the pipe is screwed into the female end. It sounds straightforward. But making and breaking joints is complicated when 100 feet of drill pipe the thickness of a man's thigh swings from a crane high above the rig floor. It's also complicated by the fact that the drilling process has tightened the joints. To break apart these lengths of pipe, the rig is equipped with giant tongs that are counterweighted so that the motorman and worm can attach them above and below the joints in opposing directions. The tongs function like 8-foot-long pipe wrenches.

I was the worm. The rig culture had not been troubled by sensitivity training. I don't think Kenny, my driller, ever called me by my given name. His face deeply lined by a lifetime of outdoor work, he always growled at me, "Worm." Or more likely, "Damn worm." My name came from my place on the drilling platform while tripping. I worked worm's corner, the back side of the drilling floor that is flanked by the giant engines. This is where the beginner begins, not because the other jobs require all that much more skill or experience, but because worm's corner is the most dangerous and dirty and exhausting place when the rig is in full action.

As the crew trips, the engines thunder and cables shudder until the joints of the drill pipe finally break free. All the power of the rig pulls in the direction of worm's corner. Because of his position between the drill pipe at the center of the platform and the engines behind, if the worm's tong breaks under the strain, or if a cable snaps, the metal crashes toward him. Working worm's corner feels like standing by the fence of the sharpest curve of a Formula One race watching the cars scream toward you, and hoping that everybody makes the turn.

My first safety lesson came when I held my tong in place as the engines began to reach toward their highest pitch. A standing worm will be cut in half by a broken cable whipped back by the pulling motors. "Crouch, you goddamned worm," Kenny screamed at me over the din of the motors. So I crouched. As the cable at the end of my tong snapped tight and I felt an unimaginable force pulse through the tong I was now holding above me with my head bowed and face instinctively averted, I had no difficulty seeing Kenny's wisdom.

The crouching position may promote safety, but it brings discomfort. Most worn-out tools clog, and the mud remains trapped in the stack of pipe that has just been drawn up and out of the hole and now towers above the rig floor. When the joint breaks free, the mud rushes out. Every trip dumps hundreds of gallons onto the drilling platform. And since that tong must be held in place as the massive cable pulls back to break the joint, I was always right there as the mud spilled out. On any given trip, I was quickly soaked to the skin. Thus did I merit my muddy name.

My second safety lesson came very quickly after the first. As the mud pours out of the drill pipe held above the rig floor by the crane above, the worm must stand, grasp the freed, 100-foot column of pipe, and force it over and against the other sections stacked against the side of the derrick. The first time I grabbed a column I was surprised by the violent, side-to-side bucking of its soaring height. The swinging momentum of the suspended steel tore it from me, and I grasped the bottom threads with my hands to gain control. Kenny almost knocked me out with a blow across the back of my head as I slid past him, carried by the shivering column of pipe across the mud-slick metal floor of the drilling platform. "Goddamned worm," he brayed at me through his toothless mouth. "Wanna lose your goddamned fingers?" He told me to bear-hug the pipe. Better to bruise your shoulder when you slam into metal and machinery than to sever your fingers. Comforting thought.

I SHOULD HAVE been miserable about the work, but I was not. When men sweat together and shiver together, they tend to enjoy an *esprit de corps.* The feeling was not unfamiliar. I had experienced it playing sports, and even more so in my fraternity of rock climbers. But what was new was the magnifying effect of machines. Dancing with dangerous and fierce iron that will both do their will and threaten their lives, men tend to form a bond that is more satisfying than the work is difficult, or maybe more satisfying because the work is difficult. And when the work of men takes them to remote, treeless plateaus to punch through the earth's skin to reach the precious blood of industrial society, they share in a secret, inner revelation of their place, their indispensable place, at the center of a sleeping world that with its calm and tree-lined suburban streets and well-timed commuter trains and smell of morning coffee turns around them in their high-spirited, splendid isolation.

No, I was not miserable, far from it. On my barstool in the Flamingo that November night, nearly three months after arriving in Rawlins, surrounded by the noise of an increasingly drunk and rowdy crowd, lost in my private reverie, I had visions of our common purpose, and I enjoyed warm feelings of solidarity with my working buddies. The music was bad and the barroom floor sticky with spilled beer. But I did not care. I was flushed with an exuberant inner embrace of everything that Rawlins had come to represent to me.

My mind was taking me back to the night shift of the day before. It had been a full eight hours, but during a rare rest before the final push to complete a trip, I sat on the end of the drilling platform with Julio, the motorman, a compact, powerful, and laconic Mexican with five small children living on the far south end of Rawlins where the new state penitentiary was being built. To our side, one of the giant heaters blew hot air across the floor of the rig in a futile gesture against the rough wind of the high plains. We were bent over our flimsy paper coffee cups that we held with both hands to draw out all the warmth they could give. We looked outward over the vast expanse of south central Wyoming now robed in noble purple of earliest dawn. In the distant semidarkness a single set of headlights twinkled on U.S. Highway 287. Immediately behind us the engines of the rig purred at gentle idle. Julio turned his face down to his coffee, blew gently on it, and then turned to me. He said in layered tones of melancholic irony and genuine happiness, "Life is good, my friend."

Suddenly I was jerked into the unpleasant consciousness of a man who had thrust himself toward me at the bar. His face was as distorted by a lust for violence as his words were slurred by bourbon. "Who you lookin' at?" he asked.

It was not an innocent question. It never has been.

I was at a loss. In high school, some boys play an elaborate game of testing taunts. In the locker room after gym class, one or two self-appointed harpies kick your sneakers across the tile floor and then stand and smirk. Other boys down the bench look silently into their lockers. Or someone knocks your books out of your hands between classes, and then says a disingenuous "Sorry." Or a group of boys who think themselves at the top of the heap decide upon a demeaning nickname. "How is our little Gomer today?"

Cold indifference can parry these probing attempts to find out where you are in the male hierarchy, but not forever. Eventually, a line is crossed, and you either submit to the humiliation, accept the dominance of those who insult, badger, and threaten, and just try to avoid them — or you enter into the ancient game of male combat that is the final arbiter of status. But my suburban high school had been pretty tame. Fighting in the hallways had been more a matter of pushing and grappling than the serious business of throwing punches with an eye toward blood.

"I said, who you lookin' at?"

"Nobody," I said. As soon as I had spoken, I realized that my answer had an entirely unintended ring of defiance. I had no idea of what I should do. The guy threatening me had no look of tentative, high school posturing. He was missing a couple of teeth. He seemed completely uninterested in the verbal jousting that might have allowed me to try my hand at the art of graceful submission. And he was miles away from the genteel Dionysian drunkenness of kids with high SAT scores on apple blossom spring evenings at Haverford College.

I saw the dirt mixed with sweat on his forehead. The flare in his nostrils sent a direct message to my gut. My brain seemed suddenly both entirely empty and completely engaged. I could hear my heart pounding and feel the veins in my neck thicken. He seemed to be saying something else, but the force of my concentration on his face and his shoulders and his hands prevented me from thinking about his words. I felt the wave of my own fear crash over me and drown whatever semiconscious democratic bonhomie I might have been feeling minutes before. I saw nothing but violence. I may have had oil-stained hands, but I was a well-scrubbed, orthodontically correct college kid who wanted to call 911.

"Hey, you gotta problem with my buddy?" I didn't turn to look, but I saw the man in front of me shift his eyes. I felt Bruce's hand on my shoulder, gently pulling me back so that he could move forward. I was suddenly irrelevant, released from the gravity of the stranger's lust for battle. Bruce never looked at me. His fierce eyes were focused on the stranger whose menace had changed complexion. My fear drained away as suddenly as it had flooded my mind. Mr. Bourbon Breath was now where I had been.

BRUCE WAS a fellow roughneck, but he was not on my drilling crew. We had met at my house, where my roommate Bob kept a constant party going. He came the first time with his brother, whom I knew only as Spider, the nickname everybody used. They were the McGehee brothers. One of the other guys smoking pot with Bob leaned over to me and whispered as he nodded in Spider's direction, "He's banned from every bar in Rawlins. Beat up too many guys." As I looked over at Spider, who had settled into a dark silence in a chair off to the side, I flinched inwardly. He was big and lean, and he looked mean. I don't recall hearing him saying a single word, and he never came around again.

Not so his brother Bruce, who smiled broadly and visited fairly often. I'm not sure why he befriended me. It amused and pleased him to make fun of my small pile of books in the room off the kitchen where I slept: Carl Jung, Herman Hesse, and other titles that would appeal to an increasingly late-adolescent seeker of my generation. Reading was not exactly a regular roughneck diversion.

But then again, Bruce was remarkable because he was not exactly a regular guy himself. He would come over to our house and sit on the couch, laughing and telling jokes. When others were talking, he would unconsciously twist his wrists, producing a loud cracking sound that I found difficult not to notice. So I asked him, "Bruce, what's with that noise?" He looked at me with a twinkle in his eye. "Well, Rusty, I was stupid enough to fall out of a helicopter upside down when I was in Vietnam, and I broke my damn wrists." "What were you doing in Vietnam?" I asked. He roared with laughter and exclaimed, "Fighting!"

There were other beer-drinking, fun-loving guys who made their way through our living room to buy psychotropic mushrooms from Bob. But Bruce's laughter blurred with passionate, serious moods. He recalled fishing with friends in his childhood in Arkansas, and his voice quivered with the joy of recollection. He had sized me up all too accurately, but with a generosity that came from not wanting to be anyone but who he was. Once he put his arm around me and spoke to me like an older brother, or maybe like a father — it was hard to place his natural combination of superiority and warmth. "Hey, man," he said, "aren't you goin' back to college where you belong?" He wasn't trying to put me down. He wasn't even trying to encourage me to leave the rigs of Wyoming, which he regarded as a place every man would savor. He meant it as a way of telling me that he liked me for who I was, which did not require me being like him.

Bruce drank with the boys, but he never seemed to be drunk. He was intelligent and he enjoyed hard work. Unlike so many of the transient personalities that drifted in and out of rig work, he had a consistency that brought him to the level of a driller, a crew boss. In many ways, he was born for success. But he was born out of season. His spirited nature, what the ancient Greeks called *thumos,* predominated. He lived by a code of loyalty, personal dignity, and love of combat. Bourgeois values of prudent self-advancement, accumulation of wealth, and reliance on law and police to maintain social order were entirely alien to his personality. From the first I judged him a good man, but I never doubted that he was a dangerous man, a very dangerous man. I was glad that he was friendly toward me, not just because he had a generous heart, but because I could see that it could be perilous to be someone Bruce did not like.

THAT NOVEMBER NIGHT in the Flamingo, with my wallet full of cash and my gently intoxicated mind full of roughneck reveries of my grand fusion with the American experience, it was my great good fortune that Bruce was not at all a man of my upper-middle-class world. He stared at the stranger. He did not try to mediate. He did not try to defuse the situation. "If you want to get to him," Bruce said, gesturing in my direction, "you gotta go through me."

The other man was silent. I thought that I could actually smell the faint but pungent and humiliating odor of his fear. Bruce was not just a linebacker of a man; he had the capacity to give his will an almost physical, visible expression in the intensity of his posture and the cold force of his voice. His eyes were filled with violence, but unlike the drunken man and his wild, uncontrolled desire for blood, Bruce's face conveyed a joyful, seemingly rational anticipation of battle.

The band was still playing in the back room. A part of my senses heard the noise of voices and the bar glasses that continued to tinkle in the sink as they were being washed. But it seemed as though the world had gone silent. The stars themselves pivoted around the gravitational force of Bruce's presence. Everybody at the bar turned. I still see their faces in the barroom of my memory. They are looking at Bruce with an awe that admires and recoils from a superior being, a god, who would both fulfill their own ideals and destroy them in their weakness.

The stranger's lips pulled back across his broken rows of teeth in an expression of primitive horror. Bruce's fierce expression gave way to a wry smile that suggested that he had known many such men and their vague, formless lust for violence, their inflated, whiskey-fueled courage. The stranger seemed more to disappear and vaporize than to turn and walk away.

"Thanks for helping me out," I said. Bruce's smile became broad, and then he laughed. "Stay out of trouble, my friend." He unconsciously cracked his wrists, and then turned to the bartender and said in a ringing voice, "Give this man a beer." He threw down some money, patted me on the back, and disappeared into the crowd from which he so miraculously emerged. It was only a couple of days later that I told my boss that I was quitting to go back to college.

A Descent in the Dark

In memory of Alex:
I never believed you would die.

I looked up as the sun struck the summits. The tops of the French Alps blazed, and the lifeless gray sky of the hour before dawn was suddenly, miraculously, vibrantly blue. Soon light was cascading down the mountainsides, and the blocky forms of granite on the mountain ridges nearby surfaced like submarines, streaming up and out of the early morning semidarkness. The avalanche of daylight swept past. In just a few minutes light swallowed the darkness in the valley below.

Colin and I were making our way down the long slope of ice that forms the bottom portion of the mountain face we had been unhappily descending all night long. With each deliberate downward step we stabbed the ice with the long, sharp picks of our ice axes, kicking in the front points of the metal-spiked crampons strapped to our heavy boots. With frequent glances over our shoulders to keep us on target, we were aiming slightly left, toward what seemed the least difficult way to get off the steep mountain face.

Now the ice slope ended abruptly. We had arrived at the edge of the *bergschrund,* the appropriately harsh-sounding German word that climbers use to describe the often large moat or crevasse *(Schrund)* that forms near the base of the mountain *(Berg)* where the glacier fanning out below pulls away from the ice face that soars above.

"This sucker looks huge," Colin groaned as he gingerly peered over the edge. I silently shook my head with the gesture of a no that really meant a reluctant yes. Colin busied himself setting up an anchor, preparing what I hoped was our final rappel — a fittingly pleasant-sounding French term that climbers use to describe recalling or returning oneself to the bottom by sliding down a rope fixed in place. "A reflexive verb," I thought distractedly as I organized the rope. "*Je me rappelle à la sûreté* — I recall myself to safety." I suddenly had a reassuring vision of my remote, serene, and confident self reaching out to bring my all-too-present, tired, and worry-battered self down the final stage of the descent.

My daydream ended as I looked up. Our traversing descent had put us underneath large, hanging ice cliffs suspended below the summit, thousands of feet above. The morning sun bathed the surrounding mountains. The distant, snowy edges of the ice cliffs above were brilliantly white in the fresh light. After long hours of darkness, the world was charged with life. My mind was drifting again, this time in a less pleasant direction. I thought for a moment about the coming heat of a sun-filled day — and of the ice cliffs melting, giving way, and sweeping down the face to engulf us. After having spent the entire night cold and lost in darkness, praying for dawn and then welcoming it, I now cursed its triumph.

I took off my gloves to fiddle with the gear and attach myself to the rope to descend. The thin prongs of the crampons rasped in the hard early morning snow as I edged into position. Aware that exhaustion was making it difficult for me to focus, I checked and rechecked the attachment of my descending device to the rope. It seemed to me that the ice cliffs far above creaked. Perhaps my mind was playing tricks. The glacier below moaned like a despairing prisoner kept in the deepest dungeon of a distant fortress. A quite real chunk of ice broke free a couple hundred feet to our right and dropped with a roar into the gaping moat below. Mountains awakened by warmth always get up on the wrong side of bed.

As I leaned out and went over the edge I could see into the dark depths of the *bergschrund.* It was filled with the debris of ice blocks that had avalanched from above. After a few feet, I looked up to Colin and said, "Goddammit, the rope doesn't make it to the bottom. We'll have to set up another anchor and make another rappel." Then down I went.

In the middle of the vertical ice face, dangling at the end of the rope, I twisted in our last ice screw to serve as an anchor. We had very little gear left of any sort; our unplanned, ill-considered descent had required us to leave a great deal behind as we engineered our way down the face. Once secured, I detached myself from the rope and barked up to Colin, "Off rappel." Hanging from the single screw, waiting for Colin to join me, I stared at an invitingly flat spot on the glacier below. We were close now to safety, very close.

COLIN AND I met at Yale in 1984. He was a first-year medical student, and I had just begun graduate study. Friends of friends of friends somehow put us in touch. During the next couple of years we went climbing on the local crags, drank beer at Archie Moore's bar on Willow Street, and spent hours talking about bigger mountains, bigger routes, and bigger adventures. It's a wonderful thing to spend a clear, cool fall day rock climbing in New England, and we had many good days. But it's something else entirely to leave the car behind and set out for thousands of feet of climbing across complex terrain to the top of a remote summit.

Climbers use a term from romantic life to describe the difference: commitment. At the local crag, if you get tired in the early afternoon or if storm clouds threaten, then you can call it quits and head home for an early beer. On a big climb it's not so simple.

The commitment is not just a matter of size and difficulty. In the mountains, weather, glaciers, and rock fall create a dangerous environment. Climbers need to move quickly, not only in order to complete a long climb in a reasonable period of time but more importantly to minimize exposure to danger. Speed equals safety, and serious mountain climbers need to be decisive, bold, and confident. There's no time for extra measures for safety.

The element of commitment is what makes for adventure. You set for yourself an objective that cannot easily be attained — and one in which failure will bring a great deal of suffering — and then you kick away the obvious supports and block the ready avenues of escape. Rather than assembling a crew on a larger, safer boat, the sailor sets out solo across the Atlantic Ocean. Rather than the sunny, gentle ridge to the summit, the mountaineer chooses the dark, dangerous north face.

These choices are mysterious, but I don't think they are unfamiliar. From time immemorial men have chosen the harder way. The term "adventurer" was first used to describe the soldier of fortune, the man who entertains the dangers of battle not in order to defend his homeland or fulfill his duty, not even for the sake of conquest and booty, but to live as one who risks death. He takes his chances. He romances *Fortuna,* confident that his skills with the sword will carry him through.

To a great extent, the basic meaning of adventure has remained constant, even as the range of activities we think of as adventuresome has expanded far beyond the exploits of d'Artagnan and his comrades. That is why mountain climbing or solo sailing or extreme skiing is not at all like the thrill-seeking of bungee jumping, or simply a matter of collecting summits. Anybody who has drunk enough beer can strap on a bungee harness and throw himself off a bridge: once you jump, it's just an exercise in screaming and letting the carnival-like mechanism do its work. As for summits, you can drive up Pikes Peak or take a helicopter to the top of the Grand Teton. Serious climbing is about getting to the top by a route that tests your competence with difficulty — and your will with danger.

A true adventurer is not foolhardy. He must realistically assess his capabilities and choose reasonable objectives. The sailor looks at himself and weighs his skills, and only then decides that he can cross the Atlantic in a smaller boat. The climber takes an inventory of his experience and judges himself capable of more remote peaks by more difficult routes. But as soon as the next step is taken, the margin of safety decreases. Bad weather, bad decisions, bad luck — all these factors crowd in more and more closely against competence and determination. That's why the best adventures involve a strange combination of emotions: a strong expectation of success in concert with all sorts of doubts and worries about the consequences of failure.

During long hours driving to and from climbing areas in the rattling cab of Colin's old Toyota pickup, we seemed always to talk about commitment. Perhaps half-aware that we were coddled Americans to whom so much came so easily, we wanted difficulties. Young and healthy, we lacked the wisdom to know that life itself would offer us plenty in due time. So, between our self-ignorance and partial self-knowledge, a general idea took shape. It might have been on the way back from the Shawangunks in New York on a May weekend in 1986. I can't remember for sure. But sometime that spring we made a plan: August in the Alps before school started again after Labor Day.

THE FIRST LEG of our trip was a grueling marathon of travel. We flew from New York to Zurich on a Tower Air charter plane packed with American students in subeconomy seating designed to extract in pain every dollar saved on airfare. But we had young backs and knees, and a striking ability to endure in the state of exhausted semiconsciousness that comes after staying awake all night. Wanting to save every possible Swiss franc, we immediately loaded ourselves and our backpacks and duffel bags of gear onto a speedy train to Geneva, where we toiled through town with our packs and bags in the midafternoon heat to get from the main train station to a suburban station. With still two more changes we zigged our way south and zagged east, and then clanked slowly up to Chamonix at the base of Mount Blanc.

We established ourselves in a European-style campground, with more than a hundred tents pitched side by side in a small field. Two English fellows, Dave and John, were set up next to us. Their ropes and gear told us they were fellow climbers, and soon enough we learned that they had spent the previous two weeks climbing rock routes on the west-facing flanks of the nearby Aiguille de Blaitière. "Great routes, mate," Dave reported, "and the brilliant thing is that the midway station of the Midi *téléphérique* takes you practically to base. The whole thing's right there. And you can get down quickly if the weather goes bad, which seems to be happening more often than not lately."

Colin and I could see the appeal, but a good night's sleep restored us to our full ambition. For us, the destination was obvious: the Argentière basin, a few miles up the valley and in the heart of the French Alps. On the south side of the Argentière glacier the summits line up in a closely spaced row: first the Aiguille de Triolet, then the Courtes, the Droites, and finally the Aiguille Verte anchoring the western end. Their 4,000-foot north-facing sides are draped with ice from top to bottom, making this compact, two-mile-long chain of mountains one of the most important places in the history of modern mountaineering. The steeper faces were first climbed in the 1960s; in 1970, Reinhold Messner opened up a new era of fast, bold ascents when he soloed the north face of the Droites. Even in the mid-1980s the more difficult routes remained a testing ground for aspiring alpinists who wanted to get to the top of the game.

We spent a cloudy day lazing around Chamonix, with John and Dave showing us the best place to buy bread and pastries. The morning that followed was cloudless and inviting. We rushed around town buying a few days' worth of food, loaded our packs, and left our extra gear in safekeeping with our new English friends. Then we walked quickly into Chamonix to take the train for the short ride up the valley to Argentière. Enjoying the scenery, we tore the grease-stained bag out of Colin's pack and ate the six *pain au chocolat* we had bought with the foolish idea that we would make them last a day or two.

In the Café Mont Blanc, which sits across from the tiny train station in the village of Argentière, I ordered my third double cappuccino of the day. While I was waiting for it to arrive, Colin gently raised the issue that, in retrospect, was to define our experience. "What," he asked, "do you think we ought to do about guidebooks?" Ever the medical student, Colin was not inclined to ignore the obvious. "Route descriptions might come in handy," he observed.

A great deal of climbing involves an almost gymnastic skill in using hands, arms, and legs to move upward efficiently. But there are complicated and important technical aspects as well. All the high-tech gear for mountain climbers has been developed in order to minimize risk. The lightweight nylon ropes and slings tied with special knots, along with an array of metal pitons, carabiners, chocks, and cams are designed to provide safety against a possible fall. The ice axe and crampons allow for safe movement over slippery snow and ice. The down-filled sleeping bags, Gore-Tex jackets, and synthetic clothing protect against the extreme weather. Our packs were full of the stuff. Guidebooks are simply another aid. They describe the routes, provide pictures from many angles, and give advice about how best to approach the bases and descend from the summits.

The waiter brought my coffee. As I lifted the cup, I enjoyed the view. The mountains surrounding us were spectacular monoliths of granite. But almost immediately I felt strangely demoralized, as I often do at the beginnings of climbing trips. Well-equipped, well-trained, and attended to by the technological achievements of modern society, the mountain climber can make big mountains smaller simply by piling up sureties against failure. The warm milk foam caressed my lips. What had seemed such a grand adventure through all our planning and preparation was now threatened by a perhaps caffeine-fractured judgment that everything was going to be too easy, too straightforward. "I didn't cross the Atlantic," I said to myself in a haughty, self-important tone, "in order to be a marathoner, treating routes as well-marked courses, and the summits as finish lines."

So I WAVED aside Colin's suggestion. "We won't need a guidebook," I asserted with an affected nonchalance. Gesturing broadly to the range of mountains before us, I said, "These are look-and-do mountains."

Colin knew my game, and perhaps silently shared my fear that our trip would be a failure because it would lack commitment. We weren't in Alaska or the Himalayas, where just the remoteness and the weather and the sheer size of the mountains generate a great deal of uncertainty. The French Alps are beautiful, but they are certainly not remote. Everything seemed so convenient, so close to civilization's protective embrace. He gave his own long look at the mountains, and then laughed and said, "All right."

After a few hours of hiking we arrived at the Argentière climbers' hut, which is anything but a hut. A large, modular building, it looked as though it could accommodate a hundred people, which apparently it does during the winter months when it serves as the first stop on a popular week-long ski tour from Chamonix to Zermatt. From tables on the long front deck that overlooks the Argentière glacier there is an intimate view of all the north faces we had come to climb. But before we arrived, the clouds had settled in, and we could only see the *bergschrunds* at the bases of the mountains across the way. The faces we had come to climb remained hidden, still hypothetical.

With my high school French I tried to explain the nature of our plans to the hut keeper. His face darkened, and he rushed off. A few minutes later, translator in tow, he returned with a sheaf of hand-drawn diagrams of new rock climbs on the south-facing cliffs just above the hut. For the next few minutes we were subjected to a litany of warnings about the horrible dangers of the north faces, alternating with a list of the virtues of the recently pioneered rock routes. "The ice is very bad this year." "There is a beautiful VIIa finger crack just behind the hut." "Last week two Swiss had to be rescued off the Courtes." "The Arête du Genepy gets the sun all day long." "Weather has been unsettled all week." "There are excellent short routes only fifteen minutes from the hut."

Dozens of descriptions lay on the table in front of us. Colin slowly collected the scattered pieces of paper, and then he patiently told the hut keeper — or more accurately the English-speaking fellow standing next to him — that we hadn't brought our rock-climbing shoes with us, just ice gear. Listening to the quick translation, the hut keeper gave us an extended and dramatic look of disbelief. Then he took the route descriptions from Colin, tucked them under his arm, and marched back into the building.

We hadn't planned to stay in the Argentière hut — by graduate student standards, it was expensive. Our packs heavy with camping gear, we made our way up into the boulders behind the hut as it started to drizzle. Eventually, we found one large rock leaning against another: a relatively dry spot for us to sit and cook.

That night and through the next day, the light intermittent rain continued. The clouds remained low, shrouding all the surrounding peaks. We sat around, cooked meals, made extra pots of pasta, invaded our cookie supply, got very bored. Another night of rain followed, and then another day. Overcome by inactivity, we decided to spend a few francs on a cup of coffee at the hut. After a couple of hours and a few unplanned but very satisfying, butter-sweating pastries, we watched as a strong wind broke up the clouds that had taken up permanent residence in the Argentière basin.

By early evening the skies were clear, and we could see the famous north faces for the first time. Their top thirds were resplendently white with a fresh layer of snow. We studied them from the porch of the hut and discussed our options. "Maybe," I ventured as I took in their magnitude, "we should do something fairly straightforward first. Then, if the weather holds, we can turn our attention to something more severe, like the north face of the Droites." We both agreed that the Couturier Couloir on the Aiguille Verte looked like the perfect warm-up route. It began as a moderate, sweeping snow slope that steepened toward the top, where the white of snow gave way to the light gray of alpine ice.

As we arranged our gear, Colin suggested that we might get some information about possible descents off the Verte. "We'll figure it out," I reassured Colin. "Besides," I said, "this will give our warm-up a little extra edge." I gave the same rationale for refusing to take a second rope, extra food, and more gear. Colin raised no protest, and we turned our attention to the pot of rice richly flavored with butter, cheese, and pieces of French ham edged with a delicious crust of oven-hardened fat.

THE DAY DAWNED perfection and the Couturier Couloir went quickly and without difficulty. We congratulated ourselves on the speed and efficiency of our climbing. "We're definitely ready for the harder routes," Colin said as we began to make our way across the narrow snow ridge that connects the top of the north face to the main summit of the Aiguille Verte. "The Droites day-after-tomorrow," I replied, "or maybe even tomorrow if we get off this route as quickly as we climbed it." But our banter turned to silence as a dense cloud engulfed us, cutting off all visibility. By the time we reached the top of the mountain, we were trying to force our eyes to see through the mist so that we could decide which of the gullies and slopes leading off the summit would take us down to safety.

We spotted a mass of nylon slings looped over a solid-looking pillar of rock — a certain sign of a frequently used fixed anchor for a descent. Since I had dismissed both a guidebook and the counsel of the hut keeper, I was forced back on vague ideas. "I'll bet that's the regular route," I guessed (correctly, it turns out). "We could go that way, but it takes us down the wrong side of the mountain. We'll end up on the Mère de Glace, and the only way back to our gear tonight will be to take the cog railway down to Chamonix, then the train back up to the village of Argentière, and then the *téléphérique* up to the Grands Montets and the hike across the Argentière glacier."

We had yet to learn that this complicated (and expensive) way of navigating through the French Alps was precisely what is required, not just for this route but for nearly all the others as well. I had wrongly balked at what seemed to me an absurdly complex and involved way to end an otherwise perfect day of mountaineering. Moreover, in retrospect, I can see that I was unconsciously making a serious mental mistake. Because we didn't have a guidebook, we didn't really know where the gulley below led. I bent the uncertainty in a convenient direction. Our success that morning was tempting me to think about a grander route tomorrow, which required a quick and easy descent to give adequate time for preparation.

We dithered for a few minutes, hoping the clouds would disperse at least long enough for us to see down. They didn't. Then I said to Colin, "You know, I have a definite memory of seeing a poster of the Verte in the climbing shop in Chamonix. I'm pretty sure that there is an easy glissade down the west side. From there we can work our way directly back to the Argentière glacier without any trouble. Let's try going down that way."

On the basis of my handy but false memory we began to descend the snow that sloped gently to the west. I was buoyed. The going was easy. But after a few minutes the slope got steeper, and at one point the clouds thinned enough for us to see that the snow dropped off below us. So we trended rightward a bit. The clouds thickened. We hit a series of deep fractures that broke the snow slope into huge blocks of disjointed ice. Eventually we dropped into one of the shallower crevasses and made our way down toward what turned out to be the edge of the summit glacier. It ended abruptly at the top of a sheer rock face.

Colin and I took council. We couldn't see more than 100 feet down the face. Perhaps we should try to go back up to the summit? We should have, but at the moment it seemed as though we had already come down a long way, and the thought of returning was tiresome. Also, I remained convinced that an easy descent lay below. So we decided to start rappelling.

We were very wrong. As Colin joined me at the end of our third or fourth rappel, the clouds gave us an opening. We could briefly see the terrain below. It was not pretty. Although the base of the face was still obscured, we now knew that about 2,000 feet of steep rock and ice lay beneath us. Colin graciously made no mention of the picture I supposedly remembered.

There was no real possibility of returning up the rock down which we had come. Continuing our descent into the difficult terrain below was the only option. Although we didn't know it (after all, we had no guidebook to consult), we were committed to going down the Nant Blanc face, a difficult route to ascend, unpopular because of its reputation for dangerous conditions, and certainly not a route we would have wittingly chosen to descend.

WE WOULD NEED to make still more rappels. The process involves doubling the rope through a fixed anchor. Climbers slide down the rope, controlling their descent by a friction device, and then they recover the rope by pulling one end down while the other snakes up and through the fixed anchor. Since we were in the middle of a face nobody descends, we needed to make our own rappel anchors by looping a piece of nylon sling over a rock outcrop, or by placing a piton or metal chock in a fissure in the rock.

After we pulled down the rope, those anchors would remain unrecoverable above. We had only a handful of nylon slings and a dozen or so pieces of rock gear, and the thought of the many rappels below made me fear our supply would be soon exhausted.

As we collected ourselves and I began counting our now precious nylon slings, a tremendous crash shook the face. Completely forgetting about the gear, I focused all my mental energy on willing my entire body into my helmet. The summit cap of permanent ice above had just shed a sliver of its bulk over the edge of the face. Ice blocks thundered down about forty feet to our left, covering us with fine crystals.

Throwing the still unknown number of slings over my head, I traversed toward a prominent rock rib on our right. Before I could think straight, I had moved thirty feet away from Colin and was clutching loose rocks and screaming, "Put me on belay!" The next volley of ice drowned out Colin's reply, giving me a Captain America adrenaline punch that quickly sent me still another thirty feet over and onto easier ground.

The rock rib put us out of immediate danger; if more ice fell down the face, it would tend toward the shallow gullies on either side. We regained our composure and began slowly climbing down the narrow spine of rock, belaying each other rather than setting up rappels and using up our limited supply of gear. "To belay" is another of those exotic technical words that climbers use — an old English nautical term for wrapping or cleating ropes to secure sails. A belayed climber can fall, but the gear that has been fastened into the irregularities of the rock, along with the rope tied to his waist and then snapped through the carabiners attached to the emplaced gear, will limit the distance and prevent serious injury. It's slower than rappelling, but since each climber is belayed as he descends, relying on the rope only for safety, all the gear can be collected by the second climber who follows the first, and thus reused later.

After long hours of down-climbing, dusk darkened to night.

We reached a snow-covered ledge. We were physically tired and mentally exhausted. "Why don't we stop here and wait out the night," I suggested to Colin. He agreed, and in silence we tried to find someplace secure and comfortable to sit.

Back at the Café Mont Blanc, I had been full of hypothetical foreboding. This trip, I worried, would be pedestrian, mechanical. Now, as I sat on the small ledge on the steep mountain face, I saw myself more clearly. In my arrogance I had brushed off the suggestion of a guidebook. Now we were reaping the consequences.

I squirmed and shifted my weight, trying to find a place where the rocks would not be digging into my buttocks. As I settled into a better spot, I found myself under an inward assault of memory. In quick succession, I saw images of Chris Robbin's body, a tiny dot 2,000 feet below me at the base of El Capitan, and then the blood-streaked rock ledge high on Middle Cathedral Rock, and then my father tumbling down the lower snowfields of Mount Assiniboine, and then Tom Kopley crying out "Oh no!" just as he slid over the edge, and then Charles Cole suddenly, tensely silent as he saw that the rope above him was nearly cut in half. I felt my heart beat more quickly as my mind replayed my own 200-foot fall in Yosemite. Down I'm going, hitting knobs of rock and desperately trying to twist myself so that I don't hit my head on the corners I know that I'll be swinging into when the rope finally goes tight — and it takes a long time for the rope to go tight.

Even now, as I write these words decades later, in the comfort of my home, my throat tightens. The memories are as fresh and afflicting as ever, and to them others have been added. From more years of climbing I'm remembering the daggers of hanging ice, the unstable slopes of snow ready to avalanche, the loose pillars of rock, the shitty belay anchors, the rappel ropes jammed, the bands of shale on mountain faces that are nothing more than stacked blocks ready to crumble. I can hear the sickening, deep whirring sound that large, killer rocks make as they tumble and spin while they fall. I can smell the pungent, acrid odor of granite smashing into granite.

And I'm thinking about Steve Mascioli and Alex Lowe and others with whom I've climbed over the years and who've died in the mountains. Why did they take the risks? Why did I? Climbing in the French Alps without a guidebook is a stupid, unnecessary flirtation with danger; but how does it differ from the game of climbing itself? I cursed myself that night on the ledge on the Nant Blanc face. I remember just as vividly cursing Steve when I heard that he died on Mount Hunter in Alaska, and Alex when I found out that he had died in an avalanche in the Himalayas. Like my insistence that we forgo guidebooks, their deaths seemed to me the dark fruit of a vain enterprise.

BUT THOSE and other reminders have produced little more than crooked branches of self-understanding intertwined with self-deception. I continue to climb. I don't doubt that I've done it for so many years because I'm good at it. It's fun to do something well.

Something more is going on, something captured in Aristotle's dictum that happiness is unimpeded activity. I dream sometimes about the wet, gray, crumbling limestone of the Canadian Rockies. I recall my parched mouth. I see in my mind's eye the long run of the rope down to my belayer. The afflicting memories return, but now they are gilt and alluring. The pain, the agonizing uncertainty, the exhaustion, the shocking realization that the mountains kill whom they will — it's all rearranged in my mind as a fire-lined gauntlet through which I have run, and I can think of nothing but the joy of running, ever faster, ever harder. Even as I curse the vain folly of bringing death so close, I long for the adventure, for the lightning flashes of self-possession, for the tremendous concentration of the will that comes from knowing that you've given yourself a thin margin for error.

This longing is not a death wish. On the contrary, I have come to see that my addiction to the risks of climbing is best understood not as wishing for death but as cursing it. God may have the power to defeat death, but I don't. My impotence angers me, as I think it has always angered men, underlying their desire for adventure. I've seen death often enough to know that she is repulsively ugly. I was not courting her on the Aiguille Verte; I was asserting against her my prerogative of life. And this act of self-assertion, it seems to me, explains the appeal of adventure.

Of course, the self-assertion is temporary, an illusion of the moment. No great ascent can cancel the car wreck that might kill me on the drive back from the mountains. No adventure overcomes the reality of divorce, the death of a child, or any of the deep mental anguish that finds its way into even the most fortunate of lives. So, yes, it's a temporary thrill. Yes, it's hopelessly arrogant. Yes, it's foolish and unnecessary. Yes, it's adolescent. Yes, it leads to illusions of grandeur. Yes, it deflects us from a sober and realistic assessment of the human condition. Yes, it's a pagan impulse. Yes, yes, and a thousand times yes. But ever since Agamemnon gathered the Greeks to sail to Troy, men have taken life-threatening risks in order to get close enough to death to give her the finger. It's a life-affirming thing to do, and it can't be done at a safe distance.

I was too young for such coherent thoughts about adventure on the snowy, cramped ledge in the French Alps in 1986. In any event, Colin was not going to give me the time for an all-night reverie, because he had come to his own conclusions. He stood up and in an authoritative tone said, "Look, Rusty, I think we ought to keep going in the dark." I hemmed and hawed, but Colin convinced me that we should not sit out the night. As long as we were going to be cold, we might as well be making headway. "You've got to get out of what you get into," he added with finality.

Colin has a way of making reasonable things sound reasonable, so I put him on belay. His headlamp began flickering below me. Maybe it was the busy work of managing the rope while belaying him, or maybe it was just the fact that we were now taking initiative, but for whatever reason my mind shifted from my inconclusive collage of doubts, fears, and memories to hunger. I thought about our stash of hard meat sausages back with the sleeping bags. I pictured myself cutting off slices flecked with large, white, glistening globs of fat.

Throughout the night we worked our way down the rock and ice of the mountain face, rappelling only the occasional steep sections where fear of falling overcame our fear of being stranded on the face without gear. Around four in the morning, when I was feeling particularly paranoid because we had only two slings and six or so pieces of rock gear left, Colin reassured me that we could always slice sections off the end of the rope to make extra rappel slings. "Great," I replied, "then we can make still shorter rappels." I had a vision of us desperately trying to reach the base of the face by making 20-foot rappels on a cannibalized rope.

OUR ROPE was still 150 feet long when I shouted "off rappel" to Colin as dawn was ripening into day and I hung on the single ice screw above the dark, hungry, man-eating *bergschrund* at the base of the Nant Blanc face. Colin came down quickly, and with another rappel we were soon relaxing on a flat spot I had picked out from above. We had made the narrow passage.

The mental tension was released, but there was no rest. We were soon on the move. Descending farther down the glacier was out of the question. Its tortured icefall would take many hours to navigate. So up a promising gulley to the southwest we went, trying to gain the lower portion of the northwest ridge of the Aiguille Verte to make our way back to the Argentière glacier and our camping spot.

When we reached the top of the ridge, we were truly and fully exhausted. Only 200 feet away was the Grands-Montets station, the top of the *téléphérique* that begins far below in Argentière. We wearily shuffled past a large party of climbers learning to use their crampons and ice axes on the gentle slopes. Japanese women in tight shorts and high-heeled shoes leaned on the rails of the station, pointing toward the horizon. Perhaps they had spotted some climbers on the distant peaks. A family in tennis shoes walked tentatively onto the glacier. As we sat to rest on the steps of the station, caressed by a calm-breathing wind, Colin and I looked at each other. After the long night of tension, fear, and concentration, the pleasant scene seemed almost grotesque. Could we really have been so isolated and distressed only hours before?

In the heat of the late morning sunshine we headed down and crossed the glacier to our gear in the boulders above the hut. I boiled water on the small backpacking stove, and made a cup of coffee that tasted like a supernaturally perfect combination of bourbon and chocolate and felt like liquid velvet running down my throat. Our exhaustion-dulled appetites awakened by caffeine, we turned our remaining food into a haphazard banquet. Colin sliced the hard sausages and cheese. I ripped open a bag of cookies, and we made meat, cheese, and cookie sandwiches, rejoicing in the fat and sugar. After a giant pasta meal and more cookies, we slid satiated into our sleeping bags.

Fifteen hours later it was raining again. We inhaled what food remained, hiked back down to Argentière, took the small train into Chamonix, and made our way to the campground to recover our extra gear from John and Dave. We suggested that they join us for dinner and beers in town. "French fries dipped in mayonnaise," I explained to Dave, "can't be beat. It packs more calories per dollar than anything else."

We made the short walk and settled into a long evening of greasy food and beer at the Bar National. Becoming more expansive with every round, we told and retold our story. Between what we described and the pictures and descriptions in Dave's guidebook, we figured out that Colin and I had gone down the Nant Blanc face in the night. "Bloody hell," exclaimed John as he compared our descent with the Couturier Couloir. "You came down a more difficult route than you went up!" Then he added with needling glee, "I'll bet you two made the first American descent."

I grabbed the guidebook from John. "Let's see if we can find something really serious for our next objective," I said to Colin with alcohol-enhanced bravado. Dave leaned back in his chair. He saw, perhaps, the perversity of our transformation of a foolish, misconceived descent into a heroic endeavor. Or maybe he was just better at holding his liquor. "The fates might need a bit of a respite before they are taunted again," he quietly observed.

But our fears were now golden memories, and we wanted more. "What about the Central Pillar of Frêney?" I asked Colin, referring to a long route on the steep, remote, Italian side of Mont Blanc, hard to get to and difficult to climb. I handed him the guidebook with my finger in the page that featured an impressive picture. He grabbed the book and studied the pages. Then he looked up, his eyes narrowing to slits. "This time," he said, "we'll copy out a route description." I smiled and raised my glass.

The Intellectual Vocation

We are currently living through a period of change in the intellectual culture of the West. During the Enlightenment and through most of the modern era, the disputed question concerned the sources of authority: What will guide our lives? Should it be the old vision of reason directed and corrected by the authority of revelation, or should we live by reason alone? Thus, Voltaire wished to strangle the priests in order to free us to follow the pure dictates of reason, and John Stuart Mill hoped to inculcate a spirit of critical intelligence so that we can overcome conventional moral categories and better serve the real needs of humanity. But times have changed. Today, the severe rationalism of the Enlightenment troubles the postmodern conscience nearly as deeply as the authority of the church. Our age increasingly regrets — and rejects — strong claims of truth, whatever their source.

In his encyclical *Fides et Ratio,* John Paul II described this new retreat from truth in pointed terms. He noted a "widespread skepticism" and "an undifferentiated pluralism," in which "everything is reduced to opinion." Overall, our intellectual culture inculcates "attitudes of distrust of the human being's great capacity for knowledge." This distrust, John Paul worried, leads to "nihilism," by which he meant a demoralized existential condition that finds the very notion of truth dangerous, untrustworthy, and illusory.

Pope Benedict XVI seems largely to share John Paul's assessment. Before his election, Benedict memorably denounced what he called "a dictatorship of relativism," the paradoxical postmodern conviction that the one thing that must be true is the impossibility of truth. Or perhaps it is more accurate to say that the dictatorship of relativism asserts something more radical: the undesirability of truth. We must quiet the commanding voice of truth so that the permissive voices of difference can be heard. Or so we are told.

Just as John Paul II worried about dangerous, inhumane tendencies in our present postmodern ambivalence about truth, Benedict foresees troubling consequences. Without the commanding truths that once disciplined and ennobled the soul, the raw imperatives of desire rotate to the center and set the agenda. We see the first signs of these consequences today. By and large the attitude of relativism underwrites a gentle hedonism, disciplined by external systems of economic reward and punishment. But it may not remain benign. Benedict returned to the dangers of a relativistic culture in his Regensburg Address (September 12, 2006), evoking the threat of violent conflict untempered by a common search for truth.

Undifferentiated pluralism, skepticism, and relativism; nihilism, egoism, and violence: one cannot complain that the magisterium of the Catholic Church soft-pedals the depth and significance of the current crisis of reason. And the forcefulness of the rhetoric is quite remarkable. Who in 1850 or 1950 could have predicted that the Catholic Church would emerge as a defender of reason in the West? But is this Syllabus of Postmodern Errors adequate? No doubt there is a pervasive spirit of relativism abroad these days, one very much reinforced by a strange new system of intellectual taboo. Yet, at least in most cases, the relativism could hardly be described as a coherent or even conscious philosophical position. Instead, it is a habit of mind, a general sentiment more social and moral than intellectual, which is why criticizing it can feel like chasing a shadow. Therefore, I think we need to carefully assess the situation we face today. Cure follows diagnosis, and we need to have a more accurate picture of how and why the postmodern West has lost its confidence in the humanizing power of truth.

LET'S BEGIN by throwing some cold water on a contemporary tendency to denounce "relativism" and "nihilism." If we turn to the contemporary university, then I'm afraid these terms do not help very much. The majority of professors are scientists of various sorts. They have a robust belief in the results of their disciplines, so much so that, in my experience at least, scientists seem largely uninhibited about telling others what is true. Part of the frustration one feels in reading Richard Dawkins comes from his cocksure confidence that the deliverances of science and his own sixty-second philosophizing can definitively settle age-old questions about God, the world, and the purposes of human life. But our exasperation should not blind us to the fact that natural scientists, even as they sometimes mishandle important issues beyond the ken of experimental method, are consistently serious about truth. No dictatorship of relativism reigns in our university laboratories.

When we turn to the humanities, the situation changes. One can always find English professors who say that all truth claims are simply projections of power or who convey to their students the new academic mysticism of alterity and difference. But in nearly all cases, this apparent relativism is linked to an agenda-driven progressivism. Instead of contributing to an atmosphere of tentative uncertainty or paralyzing doubt, those who are most ardent in questioning truth are also those most likely to ally themselves with the intensely ideological goals of political correctness. The few who describe themselves as nihilists — Gianni Vattimo comes to mind — seem to have similar, strangely contradictory profiles. The actual tone of postmodern nihilism is moralistic rather than despairing, strident rather than tentative. Instead of concluding that life is meaningless, they urge their views as a transformative philosophy that will save our culture from its supposed addiction to tyranny and violence.

If we look beyond literary disciplines, we see that, in the English-speaking world at least, the discipline of philosophy is quite removed from the relativistic gestures of postmodernism. Peter Singer can be called many things, but never a relativist. On the contrary, his utilitarianism yields a form of moral fundamentalism. John Rawls provides another example. His theory of justice may be based on impoverished assumptions about the human condition and the purposes of political life, but his basic intellectual concern is similar to the worry that motivated Benedict's Regensburg Address. Rawls sought to find a way for a commitment to reason to supervene over the potentially violent conflicts that haunt our common life. Even Richard Rorty, whose rhetoric gives the impression of denying truth, testifies to a deep moral purpose. He argued that we must give up certain fantasies about truth so that we can focus on the kinds of reasons that actually help us to live well. It's an argument that goes back at least to Montaigne and was winsomely put forward by Hume.

My goal is not to defend smug scientists, rabid utilitarians, liberal political theorists, or the deflationary humanism of Richard Rorty. My point is much simpler. If we leave aside folks such as Stanley Fish, who are more notorious than influential, then we find that the charges of relativism and nihilism largely miss the mark. Our intellectual culture may be inadequate and wrongheaded. I think it is. But the intellectual atmosphere does not seem to be either relativistic or nihilistic in any ordinary sense of those terms.

How, then, should we proceed? If we take a closer look at Pope Benedict's Regensburg Address, we can develop a more subtle diagnosis. The pope opens with a fond recollection of the community of scholarship that influenced his development as a young professor. To be sure, he had religiously skeptical colleagues. It was not as though the Regensburg faculty in 1960 was of one mind. Yet they were united in the conviction that they could (and should) discuss a wide range of questions, including theological questions about the ultimate purposes of human life. In other words, across their real differences Benedict remembers a "profound sense of coherence within the universe of reason." He worries that today this intellectual concord has been lost. It is not the case that the scientists despair of truth, or even that the philosophers and theologians have embraced relativism — although in the spirit of Matthew 7:5 Benedict has some pointed things to say about modern theology. Rather than relativism, he suggests that we have lost the confidence that the disciplines of the modern university, disciplines that achieve remarkable sophistication and produce men and women of great intellectual refinement, can come together to help us understand how we should live our lives. The total moral and spiritual achievement of our contemporary intellectual training is far less than the sum of its parts.

I find myself persuaded by this description. The crisis of reason in the West has more to do with the fragmentation or diminishment of truth than its outright rejection. We do not so much deny truth as retreat from what Benedict calls its "grandeur." The natural scientists continue with confidence. A similar spirit of energetic inquiry holds true for most social scientists, historians, and nearly all philosophers. They all manifest a commitment to objectivity and accuracy that should be cherished. Yet, while most faculty are quite confident that reason can lead us toward a genuine command of the subject matter within individual disciplines, we suspect that reason cannot guide us toward mastery of our souls — and we worry that reason cannot govern our common life in a pluralistic world. This suspicion and worry infiltrates academic culture. We are eager to convey to students knowledge of the laws of nature, social systems, and history, but we separate education from the training of conscience. Expertise with facts, we assume, is quite separate from competence in values. In this way, reason has not been denied: it has been demoralized. Our universities are less hotbeds of relativism and nihilism than places where moral and spiritual questions go unasked and unanswered.

Tracking down and refuting bad theories is a worthwhile undertaking. Skepticism and relativism are advocated by some, and they contribute to our sense that reason lacks moral competence. It is hard to give oneself over to the difficult work of seeking that which one thinks is either unattainable or illusory. The same holds for certain kinds of positivism and their unrealistic standards of proof and evidence. Restricting reason to formal proofs and experimental verification can be as much of a threat as relativism to an educational culture committed to the full development of the mind — indeed, it may be more of a threat, because our always imperfectly developed capacity for moral judgment is easily overawed by the achievements of science. Restoring the grandeur of reason will no doubt require criticisms of these views.

Nonetheless, while I concede I must also caution. Refuting bad philosophical theories and replacing them with good ones turns out to be much less consequential than one first imagines. John Henry Newman had a fine mind, yet he knew the limits of arguments. Reason, he observed, is critical but not creative. It can judge but it cannot originate. It offers analysis to the mind but not motives to the soul. As important as reason-giving is for our search for the truth, it interacts with a larger force that Newman often calls the power of "personality." Mutual sympathies, passionate loyalties, the excitement of the lecture hall, the intimacy of the seminar room, endless conversations over coffee: these and many other aspects of a vibrant intellectual community give life to reason. We are shaped by teachers who are living representatives of a past that reaches forward through them to claim our loyalty.

Although my colleagues in the natural sciences aren't likely to use Newman's term, they implicitly recognize the importance of personality. They complain about students who memorize scientific doctrines but fail to manifest the spirit of scientific inquiry. The problem has to do with attitudes, not ideas. The students suffer from the wrong habits of mind and not the wrong theories. In a certain sense, as my scientist friends recognize, students must be converted rather than convinced. They need to fall under the influence of a scientific personality.

Resistance to the influence of personality brings us to the nub of the problem. Minds need to be formed. This holds for all students, and not just those who want to go to medical school and who treat science classes as, at best, sources of useful technical knowledge to be mastered, or at worst, as hoops to jump through. A good education does not satisfy interests, it shapes them. It does not help students achieve their goals. A good education tries to give and guide their goals. This is why a healthy academic community is as much a school of desire as a school of the mind, or, more accurately, it is a school of desire because of the mind. For at its best, the mind is governed by a desire for truth, and this desire must be nurtured and directed, while other, corrupting desires need to be pruned and uprooted.

Therefore, if we return to Pope Benedict and his Regensburg Address, we can reformulate his observations. In any number of specialized domains, intellectual life is quite rigorous today. However, our communities of inquiry lack the overall personality of truth seeking. We do not cultivate the habits of mind that can help us think through broader political, moral, and spiritual questions; we lack the virtues necessary to sustain a culture of truth.

IN THE CLASSICAL tradition, the intellectual life requires the virtue of *docilitas,* or docility. Docility literally means the capacity to be guided or led. It is the virtue most directly relevant to education, because it disposes us toward our teachers in such a way that we can be properly influenced by the collective personality of culture, the accumulated wisdom that it is the job of professors to know and transmit to their students. Something about the present age seems to interfere with the acquisition and development of this virtue, and if we can achieve some clarity here, then I think we can better diagnose the current crisis of reason.

Saint Thomas treats docility in his larger discussion of prudence. It is not easy to acquire a good understanding of how to live well, Thomas observes, and therefore we need to pay close attention to the opinions of those more experienced and wiser. The virtue of docility disposes us to instruction by those wiser than ourselves. The docile mind is not overly credulous and slavishly devoted to particular individuals or schools of thought, but at the same time the docile mind is not closed to good influences. Sensitive to the ways in which the fallible human intellect needs assistance in order to make progress in figuring out how to live wisely, the docile student seeks and submits to good teachers in the hope of finding reliable guidance.

Although Saint Thomas regards docility primarily as a virtue that supports prudence, he allows that it has an important role to play in every aspect of the intellectual life. The broader application is plain to see. Even the most talented students need to be receptive to the influence of good teachers. The mathematically gifted student may be able to make remarkable progress on the basis of native ability, but in physics or chemistry, a body of knowledge must be mastered and the mind needs to be disciplined by the experimental method. This requires teachers and mentors. But the special role that Saint Thomas assigned to docility in the development of practical wisdom is suggestive, and it points us toward the troubling feature of our present age.

For the most part, we don't lack for docility in the sciences. Careerism no doubt corrupts, but students and teachers seem to possess a positive attitude toward the collective authority of the scientific community. And rightly so, for the authority of science arises from our judgment that the scientists are not making things up. They are not only well taught themselves, but we sense that scientists are — if you will permit an extension of the term — docile to the data they study. The natural scientists, we assume (rightly I think), allow themselves to receive instruction from reality. Yet in consideration of the proper ends of human action we find a very different state of affairs today. When it comes to moral questions, broadly understood, neither students nor teachers are disposed to accept the instruction of the wise, whose voices continue to live in the great books of the past. We will not allow ourselves to be taught about spiritual, moral, and political realities. We are indocile to tradition.

A rejection of the authority of the past has long been a crucial feature of modernity, perhaps the crucial feature. A great deal changes in the shift from modern preoccupations with the dictates of reason to our present, postmodern anxieties about any form of command. But there is a line that connects the rationalism of Descartes to the apparently antithetical deconstruction of Derrida. For both, and for those who come in between, the past is received as a troublesome and unreliable inheritance that must be managed by new strategies of theory. The inevitable consequence of this managerial approach is an insulation of the educated mind from the influence of personality, which is to say, the influence of inherited culture.

In the older, Enlightenment phase, the promise was that reason would take the place of inherited authorities. We will guide our lives by method rather than judgment, by deduction rather than discernment, by intelligence rather than virtue. Utilitarianism is a clear instance. It proposes to replace conscience with calculation. Postmodern deconstruction can seem very different, but it continues in the same relationship to culture. Instead of accepting the essential role of inherited culture as an agent of moral formation, postmodernity has sustained the basic form of the modern dream of reason. We are to theorize our way to a humane life rather than submit ourselves to instruction from the past. This helps explain the political urgency, the smell of dictatorship that we find in the rhetoric of relativism. The promise is simple: if we no longer believe in the good, then we will no longer have the impulse to fight over the good. In this instance, then, what seems like a counsel of despair (no stable and enduring truth) is actually the basis for us to manage our way toward a seemingly good end (a world without conflict). With the right theory of moral truth, that is to say, with the theory of its nonexistence, we are delivered from our moral problems.

The deep continuity of the postmodern with the modern project helps explain why the rigorous specialists in contemporary universities can coexist so easily with the relatively few thoroughgoing relativists. Although he firmly believes in moral truth, Peter Singer's mode of moral reasoning puts him in the same boat as postmodern deniers of truth. Both utilitarianism and the dictatorship of relativism endorse the promise of theory and method. If we have the correct theory of truth or the good or the right, or for that matter the correct theory of signs or culture or politics, then we will no longer need to enter into the laborious (and always imperfect) task of forming our consciences and disciplining our wills by way of the influence of older opinions about how to live.

To put the point as directly as possible: the crisis of reason in the West is not the result of any particular theory of truth. One can as easily be a Cartesian rationalist as a latter-day Derridian skeptic. Instead, the crisis arises out of the theoretical impulse itself. It does not matter if you are a Marxist or a poststructuralist, a logical-positivist or a latter-day skeptic, the basic educational dynamic remains the same. Theory and method take the place of culture and personality as the source for guidance about how to live.

Hegel prophetically announced this replacement in *The Phenomenology of Spirit.* Precritical men and women feel their cultural inheritance as a substantial source of truth, and they allow themselves to be formed by its particularity. According to Hegel, we have now achieved a self-consciousness of ourselves as cultural animals, and in our self-consciousness we necessarily develop a concept or theory of the process by which truths are shaped and transmitted through history. We no longer anchor our identities in substantive cultural convictions; instead, what matters now is our theoretical awareness of ourselves as cultural beings.

Thus, I don't just know myself to be an American. I know all about the ways in which national identity takes shape historically, how processes of socialization work to inculcate it, psychological factors, the "discourse of nationhood," and so forth. Hegel rightly regards this self-awareness as the defining achievement of modernity, and he affirms it as "absolute knowledge," the unsurpassable critical knowledge of one's historical and cultural identity. We see ourselves at a distance as a particular result of a larger, ongoing historical process that can be described and understood.

Few contemporary educators fashion themselves as Hegelians. His broad generalizations have been replaced by a diverse array of historical and sociological theories of culture. Moreover, the postmodern sensibility rejects the speculative synthesis that Hegel imagined would give us a complete picture of the historical process. Nevertheless, the critical shift he described and endorsed has clearly triumphed. The rationale for a revised general education curriculum at Harvard University illustrates this. "Students," we learn, "should know how to 'read' cultural and aesthetic expressions." The goal is not to convey a particular vision of life. Instead, cultural education should "help students understand themselves and others as products of and participants in traditions of culture and belief," so that they can "understand how meanings are produced and received." Cultural studies, in other words, supplant humanistic inquiry. Critical reflection, which is but a word for the acquisition and application of a theoretically sophisticated awareness of oneself as a product of culture, is the habit we encourage in students — and in ourselves. We prepare ourselves for truth by way of theories of culture, not docility to any particular culture or its vision of vice and virtue.

I DON'T WANT to give the impression that I am opposed to theories. They are powerful tools for analysis, and they play an indispensable role in holding together any sophisticated view of the world. Their importance in the natural sciences is obvious. Data collection may be fundamental in science. One can hardly explain what one cannot see. But explaining matters more. It is not enough to chart the movements of the planets. The astrologers do as much. To be a scientist one must grasp principles such as gravity. But reflective scientists are aware of the dangers of theory. Its central importance in modern science can bewitch. One can be so ravished by the cognitive power and elegance of a theory that one forgets that it serves rather than satisfies the mind's desire to know the world. This is why science makes experimental fruitfulness such a decisive test for theory. The best theories guide experimental designs that deepen and expand our intimacy with the matter under investigation. Ideally, theories intensify the power of the natural world over the mind of the scientist by focusing experimental attention. When functioning properly, scientific theories heighten the docility of the scientist to that which he wants above all to guide his mind: the natural world itself.

The single most important development in higher education over recent decades has been the explosion of theory in the study of culture. Viewed superficially, the emergence of postmodern literary theories and their broad application can be explained as an attempt by humanists to imitate the well-funded and powerful scientific disciplines. By this line of thinking, art history professors want to inject objectivity and discipline into their work. But I think a closer look shows otherwise. In the humanities theory plays a very different role than it does in the natural or social sciences.

In the sciences, theory returns the mind of the inquirer back to the material under study. In contemporary humanistic study, theory redirects intellectual interest away from actual claims that culture makes upon our souls and toward cultural processes, either those at work within the coded structures of the text (e.g., deconstruction) or cultural processes that led to the artifacts' production and influence (e.g., old-fashioned historicism or newfangled postcolonialism). In other words, scientific theory will take a young person's interest in the stars and it will sharpen, deepen, and intensify this desire to know with powerful explanations of the very reality that aroused his intellectual desire in the first place. The stargazing youth becomes an astronomer. By contrast, in humanistic study, theory induces a young person to change and redirect intellectual focus. "You used to think that the content of what you read mattered most," says the theorizing educator, "but in fact what you really need to know is how that content was produced, encoded, and made into a so-called truth that wants to gain control over your moral imagination." Theory in the humanities turns readers into so-called critical thinkers.

Consider a hypothetical undergraduate who has read Henry James's *The Bostonians.* With inchoate thoughts about the way in which James seems to commend the virtues of the parlor room over achievements in the parliamentary chamber, the student signs up for a class on James. He arrives. He is delighted to discover that the class will focus on *The Bostonians.* The works of some Marxist critical theorists are assigned, and he is asked to write a paper on the role of class identity in James. After readings in Levinas, another assignment directs attention to the Southern, Basil Ransom, as the agent of otherness. Derrida comes at the end of the syllabus, and our imaginary student, who is quite bright and quick to understand what the professor wants, develops a final paper that explains how the novel sets up a binary opposition between male (Ransom) and female (Olive Chancellor) that allows James to evade addressing the ambivalent sexual identity of the object of contest between them, Vera Terrant. He gets an A for the class and encouragement to consider majoring in literature.

I don't disdain the teaching of good theories any more than I reject the criticism of bad ones. Each dimension of the imaginary class is legitimate on its own terms. For a close reading of James's novels, it pays to gain a more sophisticated understanding of the dynamics of class identity. Levinas is well worth attention, and Derrida's methods of reading are highly relevant. As James tells us in the introductions he wrote for the New York Edition of his novels, he thought in terms of character systems, which sounds a lot like Derrida's theory of textual meaning. But notice how theory is deployed in relation to the novel in the course I have imagined. *The Bostonians* provides raw material to be operated upon and organized according to theoretical principles. The object of study is not the novel in itself but rather the cultural or semiotic processes it represents.

Again, I want to be clear. There is nothing wrong with training students to be sociologically or semiotically astute. It is good to be reflective about all aspects of the human condition. But consider the likely trajectory of my hypothetical student, a trajectory now widely encouraged in our educational culture. He starts out with an inchoate set of questions about what James had to say about good and bad ways to live, but the course syllabus works to shift his attention. What began as a moral interest, broadly understood, becomes something else. Unlike the young lover of the mystery of the stars fulfilled by a lifetime as an astronomer, the young reader who was smitten by the power of Henry James's complicated, evasive, but powerful voice does not find his first love deepened by the sort of reflection encouraged by a typical postmodern course in literature. An initial interest in the wisdom Henry James seems to convey in his allusive novels is treated like astrology, a fruitless use of the mind that only distracts from what *really* shapes the souls of people and cultures: class interests, sexual politics, textual strategies, the rhetoric of authorial omnipotence, and so forth. In this way, training in cultural analysis now takes the place of educating students about how to live.

Seeing this shift and the ascent of theory to dominance in the study of culture should help us understand the present crisis of reason, which is really a crisis of reason with respect to pressing political, moral, and spiritual questions, and not a crisis in molecular biology. According to Aristotle, the full dignity of our rational capacity is not found in our ability to solve mathematical equations, nor is it found in legitimate but subordinate moments of cultural analysis. In fact, none of the qualities of mind encouraged by our present educational culture — critical reflection, theoretical sophistication, disciplined observation — describe the highest vocation of humanity. It is politics, says Aristotle, that provides the occasion for the fullest use of reason. By politics he does not mean polling data, fund-raising, and spin. Instead, politics describes the human project of debating and deliberating about how to live.

Our capacity to undertake this project is what Pope Benedict means by the grandeur of reason. The fullest use of reason involves bringing all the real but subordinate intellectual achievements and mental habits of the contemporary intellectual life to bear on the political question, understood in the broad, Aristotelian sense, a sense Benedict sees as culminating in the theological question of what, ultimately, we should seek and serve. Culture is nothing other than the enduring form of this theo-political project, the collective effort to answer the most human of all questions: How and for what should we live?

We are not born wise. We need to be trained to think intelligently about how to live, and, as Saint Thomas points out, this requires us to be docile to instruction from those who are older and wiser. Because we need to enter into the theo-political project rather than operating upon it critically from the outside, the full dignity of reason requires us to actually listen to what others say about the proper ends of human life, and to allow their claims to exercise influence over our convictions. The same holds for the past. We must be docile to culture and the influence of its personality.

It is this disposition that we seem to lack. Our age does not want to train us to read Henry James as a person engaged in the age-old debate about how to live. Instead, we are encouraged to operate upon his work — and all other works — with a theory of culture. Therein, I believe, lies our problem. We feel the impotence of reason with respect to moral and spiritual questions, because we will not allow ourselves to be trained and instructed by the competent teachers of our tradition, or for that matter, any tradition.

AT THE END of *Fides et Ratio,* John Paul II offers a meditation on the Virgin Mary. The life of the Virgin, John Paul writes, is in "deep harmony" with the proper vocation of philosophy. Thus, John Paul exhorts us to philosophize in Mary, and he ends the encyclical with a prayer to the Virgin, petitioning her to intercede on our behalf and free us from all that hinders our search for the truth.

At first glance, the image is perplexing. One has difficulty imagining what intellectual insights the Virgin Mary might contribute to a scholarly discussion. One searches the scriptures for any evidence of important truths that the Virgin Mary can give us as the basis for our intellectual lives. So questions naturally arise. Why did John Paul not turn to Saint John and the rich metaphysical content of the Fourth Gospel? Wouldn't Saint Thomas or Saint Bonaventure serve as more likely patrons of reason? But it seems that the late pope was not interested in drawing attention to the specific teachings that faith might contribute to contemporary scholarly discussions. Instead of true doctrines or even reliable methods, in the Virgin Mary we see the perfect image of a virtuous disposition, one that is indispensable for the full development of reason. She gives herself over to the service of God's Word, which is the source and ground of all truth, and she does so without reserve. She is, in a word, docile.

The intellectual life is different from the spiritual life. We should never dispose ourselves toward teachers or books or artworks or any worldly authority with the Virgin Mary's self-abandoning trust. Our tradition has long been self-critical, and rightly so. Inspired by the example of Socrates and motivated by the ancient prophets of Israel, we have inherited a culture that teaches us to interrogate and question the claims that the past makes on our souls. Yet the critical moment is not sufficient, as the modern and now postmodern fantasy of life guided by theory encourages us to imagine. Today, we need to overcome this illusion and recover the virtue of docility in the intellectual life, because without it we cannot be instructed about how to live.

It is a paradox of culture that only the wise can reliably judge cultural norms, and wisdom itself is born out in an initial suspension of judgment that allows one to be formed by the very culture that needs to be deepened and reformed. This explains why the most profound and lasting voices of cultural renewal are those whose concern for the truth is born in loyalty. Our tears over the inevitable failures of Western culture, American society, or even the church must flow from an almost unbearable love that gives a proper and subordinate and affirmative place for the critical methods of modern intellectual life. Piety — the social form of love — infuses reason with its grandeur, for when it comes to moral and spiritual truths, we only truly know that which we allow into our hearts. Therefore, to echo John Paul, our goal should be to educate in the spirit of Mary, and our prayer should be for her kind intercession on behalf of our feeble, halting, and undoubtedly inadequate efforts to overcome the limitations of our indocile age.